CODING
FOR KIDS

*Discover How to Code With These Parent
& Teacher Friendly Activities*

SIMON WEBER

TABLE OF CONTENTS

Introduction

If asked what a core subject in school is, English, Mathematics and Science are most likely the ones that jump to mind. However, in recent years we have seen the rise of coding appearing as the new 'must teach' subject, although there is an air of controversy over whether it should or shouldn't be taught. Wherever you stand on this debate, there is no denying that learning to code can provide children with valuable skills that can be used in all areas of their life.

Even if you are leaning to code as an adult, this book is the perfect jumping off point for that much needed foundation to get you started. This book is most definitely not just for kids.

This book contains proven steps and strategies on how to start teaching children (or adults!) to code and includes hands on activities that can be used both in the classroom and at home to consolidate coding concepts, as well as useful resources to use when working with coding on a computer or tablet.

It is written in an easy to read way that even parents or teachers who don't have much coding knowledge or experience will be able to learn and teach the activities.

Chapter One

What Is Coding?

A Brief History of Coding

We think of coding as something that is relatively new, yet people have been writing code for years. Morse code, Braille and Binary are all examples of code. When you were a child you may have even made up your own secret code.

Ada Lovelace is believed to have been the first person to write computer code in 1843 when her friend designed a piece of equipment that can do calculations quickly, and Ada came up with the list of commands that told it how to work.

As this type of apparatus became more sophisticated, computers evolved, and in the 1940's powerful computers were used to help crack enemy codes during World War Two.

In the 1970s, computer coding started to be used to develop sound and graphics for games. Eventually, a code was written that allowed computers to communicate with each other, and thus the World Wide Web was brought into domestic households.

Nowadays, coding is everywhere, from the traffic light to the smartphone you use to text, and all the way to the moon on space travel.

What Is Coding?

Coding sounds daunting if you aren't technologically minded and we imagine it to be complicated jargon, which of course it is, until you understand it. In reality, anyone can learn to code, just like anyone can learn a new language, or how to play a musical instrument; it just takes perseverance.

Computer coding is simply a set of instructions that tell a computer what to do. We call it coding because the words and symbols used in computer languages are known as code.

You see, while we think that they are smart, computers are in fact useless unless somebody tells them what to do in a methodical way. The person who writes this code is known as a computer programmer. These instructions are then used to tell a computer how to run a specific program, follow a command or open an application (app). For example, when you click the button on your mouse, code has been written to tell the computer what to do when the button is clicked.

Programming Languages

There are lots of different languages used to write computer programs and this is where it becomes difficult. However, while it is helpful for children to recognize these different languages, they don't need to learn them all immediately. It is better to start with one and those who are interested can then move onto different languages as they progress.

I won't list all of the languages here, as there are far too many and it isn't necessary for a book that is about teaching children (or adults) to code, but some of the main ones include:

Scratch

This computer language was designed specifically to teach children coding, and as such it is a good place to start. Instead of typing out long lines of code, Scratch uses ready-made, colorful blocks that users put together to build instructions, which make it easy and quick once you get the hang of using it.

BASIC

BASIC stands for Beginner's All-purpose Symbolic Instruction Code. It is fairly old and is one that many people used in the 1980s and 1990s before coding and ICT (Information and Communications Technologies) made it into mainstream schools.

Java

Java was designed in 1994 and became popular because it enabled programs to run on different operating systems without having to change the code.

PHP

PHP is mainly used by coders who are working with HTML (Hyper Text Markup Language) and web design.

Alice

Alice is a free software designed by the University of Virginia. It is easy to understand and is useful for those who are interested in building 3D models.

C

This is one of the most widely used computer languages in the world and is often used to design software that needs to run fast.

It can be tricky to learn, so it is not the best programming language to start with as a beginner.

Python

This has become increasingly popular in recent years because it is short and easy to learn. There are plenty of resources available that teach Python to beginners.

Card Game Activities

While you shouldn't try and teach children lots of different programming languages at once, it is worth them knowing that there are different ones that they will come across.

Clue

A quick activity to see if they can identify different computer languages is to write down a line of code in each language onto a small piece of paper or index card. On a separate index card or paper have the name of the language along with a short clue. The aim of the game is to have children look at the programming languages and try to use the clue to identify each one.

For example, a clue for PHP might be - the name of the language is in the code.

A clue for Basic might be - each line of code starts with numbers.

This activity not only familiarizes children with different programming languages, but it also encourages them to think logically and analytically. It can be done in a classroom setting in a group or at home with adult support.

Card Match

To reinforce this learning, you can also use the cards to do a memory game by setting out the cards face down and having children take turns to turn over two cards (one name and one code) If they match, they keep the cards, if they don't they turn them back over. For younger children, it would be helpful to have the computer languages on a different colored card so that they turn over a name and a programming language or you can just put the programming names on one side of the table and the languages on the other side.

To make it easier, just use three programming languages, which would be six cards in total. To make it more difficult, add more languages.

In a classroom setting, children can work together in pairs or as a group. This promotes teamwork and collaboration, as well as thinking and memory skills.

With this activity, the code you use should be giving the same command in each programming language. The first thing that many people teach is the command for 'Hello World' and you can find this online in many different programming languages, so you can translate it into the language that you want the children to look at.

For this activity, it is better to use codes that don't look too similar, otherwise children will get frustrated and muddled up trying to decipher them. Keep it simple. There is no need for them to be elaborate and complicated. The goal of the activity is for children to see that there are differences in the programming languages.

Which Language Should I Choose?

There are a lot of programming languages, which can be confusing. The good news is that at this early stage you shouldn't worry about choosing a specific programming language right now, but instead should be more concerned with teaching the basics offline.

When you do decide to teach your child on a computer, then starting with a block based program like Scratch, or Tynker, is advisable to help them put the basic concepts you've taught offline, into a computer context.

The best way to choose a programming language once you (and your child) are ready to move on from this should be dependent upon their interest. Does your child want to build apps, for example? If so, then JavaScript or Swift will allow them to do this.

Does your child show more of an interest in building websites? If so, then CSS or HTML would be better.

Does their love lie within robotics? If so, look at Arduino.

Are they interested in Roblox type game development? If so, then LUA is a better language to learn.

Does your child love Spotify, Instagram, and YouTube? Then Python is the scripting language that is used to create these, and it is fairly easy to learn.

If you do the activities described above then you can discuss with children afterwards that different programming languages are used for different aspects of computer programming.

If you are a teacher, then you may find that you have lots of children all with different interests, so decide what you want to teach and build your learning plans around the resources that you are thinking about using. There is no point planning to teach them Python only to find out that the school is subscribing to a website that teaches JavaScript.

Whatever you choose, always make sure it is fun and interesting and that it is taught in a child-friendly way that is easy to learn, otherwise you may find your child gets frustrated and loses interest quickly.

Coding in the Everyday Environment

In the world we live in today, computers and programming are all around us and we interact with them on a daily basis, whether we are aware of it or not.

Identify Game

To teach children the importance of coding, you can ask them to identify items we use or come across in everyday life that work using computer code.

This activity can be done in a variety of different ways, both as a teacher in a classroom and as parent in the home.

For example, you can ask children to look around the home or classroom and shout out objects they can see that use code.

You can go for a walk around the local area and identify items that use code.

You can have a set of picture cards with objects that do and don't use code and the children have to sort into piles. Again, this can be done individually or as a group.

Examples of items that use code include:

Smartphones, cameras, computers and tablets, microwaves, smart speakers, smart watches and fitness bands, and other smart appliances, such as smart TV, coffee makers and washing machines. Don't forget thermostats, traffic lights, vehicles, barcode scanners, vending machines, calculators, ATM's, cars, and elevators.

There are even baby items, such as smart socks and teddy bears that monitor temperature and heart rate that all have some element of coding in them.

You can also extend this for older children by looking at industries that use computer coding, as many people think it is confined to the technological sector, and this isn't true. Coding is used in greenhouses for growing produce on a large scale. It is used in most all areas of advanced medicine. And what about factory robots? The list is long. As a matter of fact, most areas of our lives have been touched in some way by computer coding, whether we are aware of it or not.

Chapter Two

Why Teach Kids to Code?

There has been a lot of controversy surrounding computer coding in recent years, mainly because some experts have labeled it the 'new literacy'. They believe that learning code is integral to the future of the children who are growing up in the technological world that we live in today. This description has led people to argue that we *shouldn't* teach children to code because if the future workforce are all expert coders, then the pay grades for these jobs will decrease and we will end up with a pool of low paid, poorly skilled programmers.

I don't personally believe that whoever said 'coding is the new literacy' meant that it is so important it should literally replace literacy, but rather that it was just the new subject becoming popular in schools. After all, literacy is the ability to read and write, as well as comprehension skills, all of which, together with knowledge of numbers and mathematical concepts, are needed in order to understand coding.

I believe that coding does have its place in the curriculum and teaching children basic coding concepts has a lot of benefits.

A Changing World

The world is constantly evolving and adapting, and as such, school curriculums should reflect these changes. For example, when I was at school there was no such thing as phonics or literacy lessons. We were taught English and we memorized words rather than sounding them out. In later years, phonics was the new thing and children were taught to sound words out in order to read and spell.

In the world I grew up in computers were just for games and the Internet didn't exist, but now more and more businesses are relying on computer code, and not just those in the technology sector. Looking at the activities above, where we identify coding in our environment, this shows just how much we are relying on computer code and those who can write it.

Who knows what the world will look like in another twenty years. Most likely the majority of industries will be reliant upon computers, and those who can work them and program them will be invaluable.

Lack of Skills in the Software Sector

At this moment in time, experienced computer programmers are in demand and salaries can be quite high. STEM careers are going unfulfilled, so those who have the vital skills to fill these roles have a competitive advantage when applying for colleges, apprenticeships, or jobs.

Of course, by the time your child is old enough to go to work, the environment may have changed, but as coding is seeping into many different sectors, having basic coding concepts is going to be an advantage wherever they find themselves, whether it is in retail, finance, or the healthcare.

Provides a Better Understanding of the World

Do you know what makes your smartphone, video games, tablets and social media networks run? Most of us don't have a clue. When you're sat at a stoplight do you wonder how they know when to change? Probably not. We take these things for granted without actually knowing how they work. Our homes are getting more and more smart appliances, yet we don't always understand them.

Even just basic knowledge about programming can change the way we interact with technology and can mean we get a lot more out of these objects we take for granted.

Coding Fosters Creativity

With coding, kids are not just playing with technology, they get to create it and it can become an outlet for expression; whatever they imagine can come true to life. If you know how to code you can develop apps and video games, design your own website, and much more. Children let their imaginations run wild to develop something that is wholly their idea, and when they see their creation it can be extremely motivating.

Teaching Children How to Experiment

Coding involves trying and testing ideas until you get them right. Teaching children to experiment in this way can instill them with confidence. The more they get it right, the more confident they will become.

Coding is fun

Yes, coding is logic based, but it is also creative.

Learning to code can be frustrating, but it can also be fun, especially in the early days if you teach it in a hands-on way. For younger children, and those just starting out, teaching basic concepts can even be done away from a computer, so kids don't even realize they are learning to code!

Improves Problem Solving

Coding, in simplest terms, is taking a complex problem and breaking it down into smaller parts. Kids are taught to approach a problem logically and to put it into a sequence. This kind of computational thinking can be helpful in all areas of life.

Encourages Persistence

Coding is a challenge and can be frustrating, especially in the beginning when children maybe aren't used to thinking logically, and therefore make mistakes. However, persevering and making changes until they get it right is a great skill to learn. It can also teach children patience because they have to work at something until it is perfect.

Consolidates Other Learning

Children may not like standard math or literacy lessons, yet by coding they can develop these skills without even realizing it, as coding uses logic and calculation skills in a way that is engaging and fun.

It can also help with literacy skills. Some of the activities we look at later in the book will involve giving instructions in a methodical way.

Fosters Collaboration

Anyone can learn to code, and while they can do it alone, it also fosters collaboration, especially if taught in schools where kids can work in pairs or groups or at home where they can learn with a parent or siblings.

Even alone, kids can collaborate with others online. The Internet allows them to learn to work with people from all over the world; asking questions, solving problems and creating something together that can be extremely satisfying. In fact, many online games nowadays involve coding, collaboration, and participation.

Teaches Logical Thinking Skills

Computer programming isn't just about learning how to type lots of lines of code, but rather about learning how to think differently. To code you need to be a logical thinker who is able to see a large problem and break it down into smaller pieces in order to solve it in an effective manner. Clearly, this is a great skill to have and can be useful in all aspects of life, even if your child doesn't decide to have a career in computer programming.

Even if your child doesn't want to go into a career in the technology sector, or has no interest in being a software designer or a computer programmer, there is no denying that all of the above skills are useful and valuable in all aspects of their lives. Let's face it, technology is seeping into pretty much every job sector, as well as into our domestic homes, so whether your child chooses a career in retail, finance, health or any other area, these coding skills can come in handy.

What Age Should We Teach Kids to Code?

The theory is that if you teach children something when they are young, the more interest they will have when they are older. Of course, if you force coding on to them and sit them down at a computer trying to teach them lines of code that makes no sense to them, you will likely turn them off. But putting basic coding concepts into fun games and activities will enable them to learn without even realizing it. Ways you can teach coding without a computer will be explored in the next chapter.

Children's minds are like sponges and will soak information up without even trying. Experts say that kids under the age of seven can learn foreign languages incredibly fast, so should we teach children as young as two or three how to code? After all, if they can pick up a foreign language, why shouldn't they be able to pick up technological jargon – programming language?

Children these days grow up with computers and tablets and many will most likely have access to child friendly apps. Indeed, my two-year-old used to watch what we did and then copy us. By the age of three he was downloading games onto his tablet without me even knowing how he did it! I wouldn't give him any lessons on how to code or sit him down with a Scratch or Python program at that early of an age – after all he's only just grasping the English language and learning his numbers and letter sounds. While I personally think two and three years old is too early to teach children to code, I do believe that by age four or five it is possible for children to learn basic coding concepts away from the computer, as well as on certain apps or software, with supervision.

Basic Coding Concepts

The following are basic concepts that you can teach children as young as four or five years old without even the need for any technology.

Algorithm

An algorithm is a set of step by step instructions for performing a task or solving a problem.

Sequence

A sequence is the order of steps in an algorithm. These steps need to be given in the correct order. If anything is out of sequence, then the task won't be performed properly.

Events

An event is an action or occurrence that a computer recognizes and has specific instructions on how to react to a certain event. For example, if you click on the mouse the computer may respond by opening an app or a game.

Conditional Statement

This tells a computer to do a certain action that is dependent upon a specific event. For instance, let's say you type in a certain command in the search box and press enter, or use the mouse to move the arrow and click it on a certain icon - this might result in the computer opening a specific program. If you don't click the mouse or press the enter key, then the computer won't do anything.

So, we can describe the conditional statement for this above example as something like:

IF I press enter THEN the computer opens this program.

IF I don't press enter THEN the computer does nothing.

These simple conditional statements help make up the complex programming algorithms that we use every day, often without even noticing it.

We can teach these statements using real life examples to make them real to children and to teach them to think logically about every day occurrences. For example:

IF we keep put water in the freezer THEN it will turn to ice.

IF we take the ice out of the freezer THEN it will turn back to water.

IF it is hot THEN we wear sun-cream.

IF it is not hot THEN we don't wear sun-cream.

Conditional Game

Move on to asking children questions for them to finish. For instance:

IF I make a loud noise when you are asleep THEN….. (You will wake up)

IF I don't make a loud noise when you are asleep THEN….. (You will stay asleep)

16

After giving a few sentences for children to finish, ask what will happen if... and then give some examples, such as what would happen if it does rain/doesn't rain? What happens if we do turn the TV on/don't turn the TV on or other similar questions. Ask children to give an If/then statement depending on these examples.

Finally, once children have grasped the idea of the conditional statements, ask them to come up with their own. If you are teaching this in the classroom, then when you introduce the concept for the first time you can put children in pairs or groups to come up with their own cause and effect scenarios in order to build their confidence.

Read out the conditional statements. If some statements are not quite right, try to come up with ways it can be changed in order to make it correct. Discuss why it isn't right and then try to solve it together.

This activity will teach children logical thinking.

Loops

These are common computer science concepts that are used in most programming languages, although they might look slightly different depending on which one you use. These loops enable a condition to continually be followed until something happens to stop it. For example, in a farming game it might be that plants are growing while it is daytime. In a zombie game, it might be that zombies are roaming around whenever it is nighttime. These are examples of loops that continue looping over and over until something stops the loop.

Why is Python The Best Choice For Kids?

Python is hands down the best and easiest computer programming language in the world to learn. Compared to many of the other computer languages, the syntax and the commands in Python are much simpler to learn and this, alone, makes it so much easier for a child to learn, even with little or no coding experience at all. Plus, because Python has so many libraries that are easy to import when we need them, it is an incredibly flexible language – and you can even import libraries by others to create some unique and fun projects.

Chapter Three

Offline Coding

Nowadays, it feels like babies are born with the ability to work a computer. Indeed, my youngest child was able to download apps and play them by himself by the age of about two and a half, simply by watching his older brother and copying what he did on his tablet.

However, I wouldn't recommend sitting a child as young as two or three down in front of a computer to teach them a computer programming language and expect them to pick it up. Indeed, even with older children it is far better to learn the basics in a way that is hands on. In fact, you don't even need a computer to teach children the basics of coding. I know, it sounds crazy, right? Offline coding allows children to explore the concepts in a way that is fun and allows them to process it in their own way, relating them to real life experiences.

Another benefit of offline coding is that you can add these experiences into their everyday lives or in a school setting. They can be an added dimension to, say, a mathematics or English lesson.

Offline coding can get a child interested in computer programming that may not otherwise want to sit in front of a computer and look at jargon for hours on end.

Plus, there's no guilt about how much time children spend in front of a computer, which means you can add in coding experiences more regularly during the day or week and children don't even have to know that they are learning coding unless you wish to tell them.

Preschoolers

I will add in a note about preschoolers here because even though parents often say they aren't going to let their toddlers use computers or tablets, there is no denying that some of these products are becoming geared toward this age group. I'm not going to go into the pros and cons of it or start a debate about whether a two year old should be bought a tablet or not, but I do believe there are benefits if they are used in moderation.

While I didn't grow up with a computer in my hand, I feel that my children's generation is being brought up that way and that it does benefit them to know how to use computers; the future is becoming more and more technology based and, therefore, their generation is going to be engrossed in it.

Computers weren't really used when I was a child, so as a teenager we were taught the very basics, such as how to turn the computer on, open Word Documents or set up a spreadsheet and so on. While this may still be taught in ICT lessons, I think the presumption is that most children understand how to turn on a computer and open a program. Tablets are becoming more common in classroom settings and I can only presume that eventually it will be assumed that children can do the basics and what is taught in schools will start a bit further along, therefore teaching them at a young age at home means they won't be at a disadvantage.

Again, this doesn't mean I would recommend sitting down a toddler and teaching them Scratch or using computer jargon with them. You aren't physically going to teach your toddler and preschooler coding, but you can teach them logical thinking and problem solving, which are skills needed for coding, and this can be done with inset puzzles and floor puzzles. These are in essence problem-solving tasks that allow children to examine smaller pieces to make a bigger picture; a foundation of coding is the ability to break a big problem down into small steps.

Tangrams

Tangrams are also great for exploring shapes and solving problems; can children make a certain shape or picture? You can start by getting younger children to match up the shapes to a board and talk with them about what the picture is. Then move on to have them copy a pattern or picture that you make. Then have them making up their own pictures and patterns.

Building Blocks

Building blocks are also a great toy for budding engineers and computer programmers. After all, building something out of blocks takes a lot of determination and patience, especially for a toddler who is just starting to refine their motor skills. It also requires logical thinking to figure out how blocks can be placed, which pieces fit on top of each other, and which ones don't. If it topples they have to rebuild it, but work out a way that they can do so without it falling down again. Learning patience will be an extremely helpful skill in for coding.

Dominos

Domino chains help children to understand cause and effect. Stand the dominoes on their sides to make a line or a pattern on the floor; what happens if one falls?

At this age and stage of a child's development you don't even need to relate it to coding and computers, you are just trying to instill patience and logical thinking for the future.

Games like Simon Says, Mother May I?, as well as board games can help children think logically and follow instructions.

Reading stories can help preschoolers understand sequencing.

These types of toys can be used for teaching older children just by extending them, which will be explained in more detail later.

Mazes

Mazes are a great way to teach children coding concepts. The rules for these mazes are that you and the children have to use coding language.

Chalk Maze

This is a fun game because it can be done on a large scale, depending on how complicated you want to make it and how much space you have available. Chalk is great because you can draw on the driveway or sidewalk or school playground and eventually it will wash away.

Draw a six by six square grid. If you want to make it larger or smaller then you can do so, but this is a great size to start with.

Next, you need to color some of these squares in. If you are at home (and it is a warm day outside) then you may want to make these 'spray zones'; if the person in the maze lands on these squares then they get squirted with water or sprayed with silly string. The aim of the game, therefore, would be to guide the person to these zones because it is fun to spray them!

Of course, in a school environment this may not be appropriate, so instead of water you can throw soft sponge balls or you can color these zones red and tell the children they have to avoid the red squares because they are 'lava' or you can draw in crocodiles or sharks in some of the squares; if the children land on these they have been 'eaten'.

Once you have decided what the goal of the game is then you can start to play.

One person is in the maze and they are the 'robot'. If you are doing this with young children it may be better for the adult to be in the maze. If you are doing the spray or throwing balls, then the goal of the game is for the person giving instructions – the 'programmer' to direct the 'robot' to the squares you colored in. If you are using 'lava' or 'shark' squares then the aim of the game is to avoid these colored squares.

The 'robot' can start anywhere on the grid. The 'programmer' gives instructions and the 'robot' moves accordingly. However, the instructions have to be given in computer code.

For example, the programmer might say 'Take 3 steps forward, turn, two steps forward, turn'.

You can change the difficulty of these games depending on the children's age and ability.

The easy version is that the robot can only move forward and turn in one direction.

A medium difficulty level would be to have fewer colored zones if avoiding (or more if the aim is to land on the squares). The robot can now move forward, backwards, left and right.

The harder version is having fewer colored zones (or more if the aim of the game is to avoid these squares). Children have to work out the whole maze and give all the instructions in one go. For this you may need to give them pencil and paper so they can write the code first.

If an instruction isn't correct, then children can go back and 'debug' their code by working out what went wrong.

This harder version works well in schools where children can work in small groups in order to work out the code in advance and debug it.

Learning Outcomes

This game teaches sequencing, as the instructions have to be given in a specific order, otherwise the outcome won't be correct.

The problem solving is when the children are working out how to get the 'robot' to a certain place.

It also introduces basic concepts of coding, such as directional language.

Blindfold Maze

You may find that older children try to work out the maze for themselves rather than following instructions, which misses the point of the game. A good way to get them to listen carefully is to blindfold the child who is in the maze. Younger children may not like being blindfolded which is fine; you can ask them to close their eyes instead or look down at their feet, but I have found that younger children don't tend to try to work it out for themselves, as they find it more interactive to be given instructions and they don't always have the capacity to think so far ahead anyway. If they do try to run quickly through the maze, then you can make a joke of it – "Oh no, the robot needs debugging" and get them to start again and listen.

Make a maze out of cardboard tubes, Lego, or other toys. I have seen this called 'Don't step on the Lego' maze, however, knowing firsthand how much stepping on Lego actually hurts, I wouldn't recommend attempting a Lego maze in bare feet! If you want the person in the maze to know when they've gone wrong, then you can make it out of popcorn or bubble wrap or something else that makes a noise when you step on it. If you decide to do this outside, you can use crunchy autumn leaves. Another way of letting them know when they step outside the maze or on the boundary line is to have a buzzer or bell or something that makes a noise; when they hit a boundary line or head the wrong direction, it makes a noise, so they know to stop, then give them different instructions.

Whoever is in the maze is the 'robot' and the person giving instructions is the 'programmer'.

The 'programmer' gives instructions (an algorithm) and the 'robot' follows these. For instance, you might say forward three steps, turn, one step backwards, turn'.

As above, you can change the difficulty level by introducing left and right and backwards or by giving several steps at once, making it harder to think ahead (which is an essential coding skill).

If the 'robot' steps on a maze line, then it has to be 'debugged' and start again from the beginning.

When you are doing this at home, it can be frustrating for young children to keep starting again, so it may help if you write the instructions down as you go along so that you can swap over and 'debug' together when they are first learning these concepts. Again, in a classroom situation, children should be encouraged to work together so that their frustration is managed, and they aren't as stressed if they make mistakes.

Learning Outcomes

If carried out blindfolded, this game teaches listening skills, as well as how to follow instructions. If the child is the programmer, it teaches them to correct mistakes ('debugging') and how to give instructions in a sequence, and to think logically.

If this is carried out in a school setting or with more than one child, then it also teaches collaboration, as children can work together to problem solve.

Egg Box Maze

This works really well if you have those large trays that hold lots of eggs; usually you get them if you buy eggs from farm stores. If not, you can open smaller egg cartons and tape a few of those together so that you have a large grid. Remember that the more egg cartons you use, the bigger the grid will be and the bigger the grid, the harder the game. If you have younger children who get bored very easily then just taping two egg cartons together so you have a 12-hole grid may be adequate enough for their concentration span. If they enjoy the game and want to play again, then you can add more egg boxes.

Once you have made your grid, put some plastic eggs with sweets or chocolate inside. These are your 'surprise eggs'. You can also use Kinder eggs or small chocolate eggs if you prefer, but I find the plastic ones are super cheap and of course you can refill and use them again, which makes the game less expensive, as you don't have to keep running out and buying new ones every time you want to play.

Spread the eggs out in your grid so they're not all in the same row or grouped together. Scrunch up some red or grey tissue paper and place these in some of the empty holes. (If you use grey paper they can be rocks, red paper can be hot lava). Next, find a small toy to move around the grid – this can be a mini figure like the sort you find in Lego or Play Mobil, or it can be a small animal figure, or something similar.

The aim of the game is to get the figure through the maze to collect all the eggs, but avoiding the rocks or lava. As this game is fairly small scale compared to the ones described previously, it can be played at a table or on the floor and can be played alone if doing it at home once the child understands the rules.

To move the figure around, first you need to write instructions as an algorithm. It is easier for the child to write them down as you can then check to see that they are correct, and they are following them closely. Sometimes children have a tendency to cheat just to get to an egg if they are playing alone, so I always tell my children to write down the algorithms and then I watch them follow the instructions or else I will follow the instructions they have written down and if correct, I give them the egg. For instance, they might write down move two spaces, turn, move forward three spaces, turn, move forward one space. This then takes them to a certain egg.

As mentioned above the larger the grid, the more difficult the game. More eggs will also make it easier, fewer eggs make it harder, likewise more rocks make it harder, less rocks make it easier. As with the previous mazes, you can also alter the difficulty rating by the type of instructions you allow; for example, younger children can just say turn and move forward. Older children can have left and right and forwards and backwards introduced.

I would recommend for young children just learning to code that you make it easier and adjust the difficulty level each time they do it. For older children or those working together in pairs or groups then you can make it more challenging.

In a home setting, it is fun for the child to work with the parent or sibling, but as mentioned above, you can leave them to write the algorithm, then you join in at the end or you can write it together. Once children are confident in what they are doing, you can even have one large maze and let children work out their own instructions separately. For example, one child can aim to get one colored egg and another child can work out the algorithm to reach a different color, then they can swap paper and each follow the other person's instructions.

Whether working in a home or school setting it is important that children understand what is expected of them, so it is always a good idea to model the game first. This can be done by you writing out the instructions first, and then demonstrating how to move the figure. Or, you can write the instructions and move the figure together.

In a school setting, children can work alone or in pairs or even as a group of four or six. Again, you can have a different maze between each pair or just have one large grid on the table for each child to work out their own instructions.

If children make a mistake they can go back and try to work out where they went wrong, re-writing the instructions until it works, or in other words, they can 'debug' their mini figure.

Learning Outcomes

Children will learn how to write algorithms, as well as how to follow instructions that are written in code. If working together, they will learn how to collaborate and listen to one another. If they make mistakes they can learn how to alter these, which teaches perseverance and problem solving.

Lego Duplo Maze

Lego is a great toy to use for mazes. You can use Duplo to make a large maze on the carpet or small Lego pieces for a smaller table top style maze. If you are using the smaller table top type maze, then if you have any of the base plates these are great to use, and you can make larger mazes by joining base plates together. Of course, if you are doing this with a young child, then Duplo is more suited to their age group; smaller Lego tend to be aimed at children aged five and above.

To do this activity, make a maze with the child. Older children can have it modeled and then make their own or they can design a maze on paper first. This works well in a classroom setting, as it gets children thinking and planning and allows the teacher to walk around and give input to individuals if necessary. You can even allow every child to design a maze, but then put children in groups where they can select one to make. If they have time they can then make someone else's maze.

Younger children can have the maze made for them, but help by adding fences and other bits and pieces once the main outline has been completed to give them a sense of ownership, and let them feel like they have helped.

Once complete, you will need a figure or small toy to move through the maze. If you don't have any Lego mini figures or animals, then just a small toy like a dinosaur will suffice. You can use a small car, but be aware that children may just push the car forward until the end of a path or negotiate the maze with it without listening to instructions, therefore I would probably avoid cars and use a person or animal type figure that they can just 'hop' up and down as you give instructions like 'move forward five steps'.

Once children have the hang of giving and following instructions for the maze verbally, you can extend the activity by getting them to write instructions themselves. For younger children, this can just be a case of drawing arrows to show the movement; so three arrows in a row would mean moving three steps forward; an arrow pointing left would mean turn left. You can help them set these out and then move the figure following the arrows they have set out. You can draw these directions on small pieces of paper and just have them lay them out or you can get them to write them themselves - this purely depends on the child's ability.

Older children can write instructions for themselves and then you as a parent/teacher or another child can try to follow them.

It is important that you model what you want the child to do so that they are clear about what is expected of them, but as with all these games, let them make mistakes. Don't correct them until you (or they) are actually testing out whether it works. Trial and error is all part of the learning journey.

If you set out the instructions, then feel free to get it wrong as well. Can your child correct your mistakes? Children love it when they can point out an adult error and again, it helps them check things thoroughly and gives them an eye for detail.

Learning Outcomes

Again, this is all about listening and carrying out instructions, as well as giving them. It is about correcting mistakes; all programmers will make errors, but spotting them is what makes them good at their job. These maze games also teach children to think one step ahead and plan their actions before carrying them out.

Themed Maze

What I love about offline coding activities is that you can pretty much design them to suit any interest and can add them into other lessons. A lot of schools have a theme every half term so you can even organize your coding activities to match this. For instance, sometimes in the younger age groups the theme might be related to a book, such as The Hungry Caterpillar or fairy tales like Goldilocks and the Three Bears and so on.

I loved the Hungry Caterpillar type coding activity because it is easy to set up. Basically, you just need a cardboard caterpillar, which you can get children to make in an art lesson if you want to and some cardboard or plastic food.

Scatter the food around the carpet or on a table and then give the children some cards with arrows on. The aim of the game is for the children to make a path to the food for the caterpillar to follow.

Once they can do this confidently, you can start to add in obstacles for them to negotiate around.

If you do Goldilocks and the Three Bears theme, then have a doll for Goldilocks and cardboard bowls (or bowls from a toy tea-set) of porridge for her to collect. If your children are too old for these, then you can have a robot collecting nuts and bolts, monster truck running over small cars, garbage truck collecting trash (balled up pieces of paper) and so on. Really, your only limitation is your imagination.

For older children, they can write out the directions and work it out before they put it into practice. Talk about de-bugging if they get it wrong.

Minesweeper Offline

Did you ever play Minesweeper when you were a kid? Back in my day, computers had very limited games programed into them and we would spend many a break time at school staring at a tiny grid, groaning when we hit a bomb.

You can replicate this game at home without a computer. If you have a tiled floor, then this is great because this serves as your grid – each tile is one square. Simply cordon off an area to use as the 'game board'.

If you don't have a tiled floor don't despair, you can use sheets of paper or playing cards. Whatever your using, lay out your grid first, then draw a grid on your paper replicating this. If you are using playing cards and have set out a 4 x 4 grid (16 cards in total), then draw a 4x4 square grid on your piece of paper.

Next mark out some squares on your paper that are your 'mines'. The aim of the game is for the child to avoid these. You can let them play randomly and then work your way up to guiding them through the grid avoiding the mines.

Once they have the hang of the game, let them draw some of their own maps and guide you.

If you are playing on tiles, then your child can simply hop from one tile to the next. If you are using playing cards, they can just use a small toy to move from one to another.

If they are hopping randomly, then you can still give directions or clues, such as miming if they are 'hot' or 'cold' so if they step on a square and one of the squares next to this has a 'mine' then you can mime being hot, such as fanning your face. If there are no mines nearby then you can mime being cold, such as shivering.

Learning Outcomes

Again the learning outcomes are giving and following instructions. Giving directions in a methodical manner, but also planning these out in advance. When they are guiding you through the maze they need to place the bombs in places that still allow a path through the maze that requires logical thinking.

Story Sequences

This is a fun game and can be done as part of a literacy lesson if you don't have time for a specific coding one. It involves breaking down a story into small sections, mixing them up and then getting children to put them in the correct order.

For younger children, it is better to use a story they are familiar with to give them confidence. Pictures are often more fun as well and allows them to study each one for clues as to what goes where.

For older or more capable children, you can use pictures that are similar, but where certain details are changed to show which one is first. For instance, it can be as subtle as a time on a clock or a person wearing a coat. Children have to have an eye for detail to spot these changes and work out which order the pictures should be put in.

Learning Outcomes

This game teaches sequencing, which is an important skill when understanding how to code. After all, if you cannot get a sequence correct then the computer will not do the task it has been programmed to do correctly, as it will have been told to do it in the wrong order.

Food Preparation

This is a fun way for children to follow a set of instructions in the correct order and highlight what happens if the order is wrong. It doesn't have to be just following a recipe, but can be as simple as making a sandwich. It is amazing how when we do a simple task we don't actually think of how many steps are involved nor do we think about the order in which we do them. We simply automatically do things to make the task easier, but when it comes to breaking it down it is easy to forget steps or get things out of order.

For young children, just letting them follow the recipe is enough. You can use pictures at each step to make it easier, and if you wanted to extend the activity then you can help them order these beforehand. For instance, a picture of a mixing bowl, rolling pin, measuring jug, etc. shows them that they need to get these things out. A picture of weighing scales next to a bag of flour to show they need to weigh the flour and so on.

For older children, you can simply have them tell you what to do and you follow their instructions, so if they miss steps, it highlights what happens if things are out of order.

For example, if they say, "Butter the bread" but haven't told you to get out the butter or the bread then you just stand still. If they tell you to get out the butter and the bread and then say butter the bread but haven't told you to get a knife or haven't told you to take out two slices and butter them separately then you can pretend to butter the whole loaf with your fingers or ask questions such as, "What shall I butter it with?" or you can just be silent and still until they realize what they need to say first. Just be aware that some children may find this silence frustrating, so you may have to pre-warn them that you 'won't work' if things are in the wrong order. Personally, I find trying to do what they have told you to do is far more fun and it makes it sink in.

When children are incorrect, they can go back and correct this or if you are being a computer they can 'debug' you.

You can also do this in the reverse order, with the child following instructions. Do they do things without you telling them to? If so, highlight this. Give some instructions out of order on purpose so they can see what happens if the steps aren't logical and let them tell you what is wrong.

Learning Outcomes

As well as sequencing and logical thinking, this activity demonstrates why things need to be broken down into small steps and put in order. It challenges children to think about what happens if things are in the wrong order and why it needs to be correct. For example, if out of order, then the end result isn't right. You can't stir a flour and egg mixture if you haven't got a bowl out first. There's no point putting cake mixture in the oven if you haven't turned the oven on. If you put cake mixture in the oven, it needs to be put in a tin, not the bowl it was mixed in and so on.

It also teaches children to go back and alter things, allowing them to learn from their mistakes.

If the child is pretending to be the computer, then it also improves their listening skills.

Ready to Leave the House Game

This is similar to the game above, but far less messy!

If you are doing this at home with just one adult and one or two children, then you can use a doll or a teddy bear, but if you are doing this game in a classroom setting then you can choose one child to be the one 'getting ready'.

The scenario is that the teddy bear/doll or child is getting ready to go out, for instance, to school or to the shops. What do they need to do?

You can lay down the doll or whatever you are using and pretend that they are in bed. Can the children break down the steps of getting ready? For instance, this might be get up, have breakfast, clean teeth, get dressed, pack bag, put on shoes and leave the house... but can they break down each of these steps into smaller ones? For instance, what does having breakfast entail? Getting the cereal bowl out, getting a spoon, pouring the cereal, getting the milk out of the fridge, pouring milk, putting the milk back in the fridge and so on.

You can make this game lots of fun by being overly dramatic if a step is wrong. For instance, using the example above of getting cereal, the children might say pour cereal but not say get a bowl out so you can groan and say something like, "Uh oh, there's cereal all over teddy bear's floor now." The more over the top you are the more children will love it and it demonstrates what happens when the steps are out of order.

If you are doing this at home one on one, then the adult can be the doll or teddy bear and then you can swap. When you are the one giving instructions, get it wrong sometimes so your child can see what happens if things are out of order and work together to solve the problem. For example, if they say "Put your trousers on" but don't tell you to "Put your leg into one of the trouser legs" first then you can put your trousers on your head. What is wrong? You've 'put them on, right?' Children will love this sort of silliness and will take great delight when it's their turn to do the same so make sure when you are giving instructions you get things out of order or miss steps out too!

If you want to make this more visual for younger children you can even have cards with pictures so if they are not sure they can look at it and order the cards first. This can also be a follow up activity in a classroom setting for children to do individually or in pairs.

Learning Outcomes

This can be such a fun game, especially for young children. Just like in the previous game, it teaches them the importance of giving steps in the right sequence. It also teaches them to break down a simple task into small easy steps and shows them what happens if something is missed out. It can help them be methodical thinkers as well as great problem solvers.

Steps in a Computerized System Game

For older children you might find the 'getting ready' game a bit too simplified, or you might do this or the food preparation game and want to move on to something more complicated. A game that has similar learning outcomes, but is more challenging is to think about the steps in a computerized system; this can be a set of traffic lights, an automatic till in the grocery store, a vending machine and so on. What are the steps that make it work? You can allocate the item based on that children's ability. For example, the higher the child's ability, the more complex the system. You can have children work in pairs or in groups and have more than one working on the same system. If you are working at home then the adult can write down the steps as well as the child.

When everyone has completed the steps, you can take it in turns to read out the steps and compare it to someone else who has the same system. Did they both write down the same steps in the same order? Has anyone missed a step? Discuss which was right and why. This is a great way for children to start spotting mistakes.

There are two ways you can complete this activity. For less able or less confident learners, you can give out cards with each step on it. These can be written in short sentences or can be picture cards. Make sure they are shuffled so they are out of order. Children can look at the cards and discuss which goes first, which is next and why they think that to be true. This is great for those children that don't think they understand computerized systems and struggle to understand what is actually required of them.

Learning Outcomes

Again, this is about thinking about something logically and breaking each event down into small steps. Can a vending machine drop an item out without a number being put in? What happens when someone presses the button to make the machine work?

The difference between this game and the ones listed above is that children are actually thinking about a computerized process and the mechanics involved, which in turn helps them realize how complicated even the simplest machine can be.

Working in pairs encourages collaboration, and comparing work allows children to spot mistakes in other people's work or in their own. It helps for them go back and learn from these scenarios.

The Impossible Question

A Fermi question was named after the Nobel Prize Winner and Physicist, Enrico Fermi. They are questions that are difficult to answer. In fact, we cannot really ever know the correct answer, but the point isn't about the exactness of the answer but rather the steps we take to answer it. The importance is the process as to how you arrive at the answer rather than the answer itself.

For example, you may ask, "How many times can somebody say the alphabet in forty-eight hours?" To work this out, you may ask how long it will take for someone to say the alphabet once. You can time this, but of course, it may be different for each person because we all speak at a different pace. Let's say somebody can say the whole alphabet clearly in six seconds. How many times is this in a minute, then an hour, then twenty-four hours then forty-eight hours? You can give an answer to this, but of course, it would vary, therefore there is no exact answer that would be correct. For example, for someone who speaks faster, the time would be less; for someone who speaks slower, they would say the alphabet fewer times. Are they constantly saying the alphabet over and over or would they have a break, say if they are eating or sleeping? Therefore, children are encouraged to think and ask more questions. The only way we would know the exact answer is to carry it out, and is anybody going to do this? No, therefore, we have to estimate it using logical thinking to give the most likely answer.

Another question that is far more difficult to come up with an answer can be how many balls would it take to fill the school auditorium? Again, how big are the balls? Are they tennis balls, footballs, or basketballs? How big is the school auditorium? Is it empty or are there chairs or a stage in there that need to be accounted for? Again, the children are questioning rather than answering. They don't have to physically go and measure the auditorium; they just need to ask the questions to determine what criteria would change the answer.

It is fun to discuss everybody's answers to see how they came up with them. Did anyone give an actual answer and if so, was it the same as anybody else's? What questions were asked and did everybody ask the same ones or did they come up with something different? How would we begin to tackle such theoretical questions?

Learning Outcomes

The impossible question may seem to be a pointless question, but it's actually encouraging computational thinking. In coding, people need to ask questions and think about the logical answer. It is teaching children to think about all the variables in a scenario and shows that not everything is straightforward and linear.

If/Then Games

These games are based on conditional statements.

Hula Hoop Game

This is super easy to set up and can be done outside or indoors, and it works well in schools where they tend to have lots of PE equipment. At home you can do it on a small scale using either pieces of card or making circles out of Glo stick necklaces. For the purpose of explaining here, I will assume you are using hula hoops.

Spread out the colored hoops so children can easily step from one to another. Choose someone to be the 'programmer' (again you can have more than one programmer so children can work together, which can give children confidence, especially in a school setting). The children in the hoops are known as 'computers'; when the programmer(s) shout out a color, the other children have to listen and move. For this game, more than one child can be a 'computer' and move at the same time. For instance, the programmer(s) may shout out something like "IF I say BLUE then go to the BLUE hoop" and the children will then race to find a blue hoop.

Another way of doing it is to put children in a different colored hoop. The number of children you put in at a time depends on how many hoops you have. Let's say you use four children. Put the kids in different corners, then the 'programmer' can say something like "IF I say BLUE, move until you reach a BLUE hoop" the 'computers' then have to move to a blue hoop, stepping in one hoop at a time and turning if necessary.

Make it more difficult by telling children they have to find the right colored hoop in as few moves as possible. You can even specify this. For example, you can only step in five hoops to reach a blue one; this means that rather than running around manically they have to actually think logically about where they are moving. You can also add in extra conditions, such as they can't step in a hoop that another child is in.

If a child doesn't follow instructions properly in both scenarios, or the last child to find a hoop is out, you can make this computer related by saying they need to go to the repair shop to be debugged.

An extra challenge is to give the code using claps instead of statements. For instance, three claps means the children move to a blue hoop, one clap means they move to a green hoop, two claps mean they find a yellow hoop and so on. If you have more than two colors, then it may help children remember by writing them on a board or large piece of paper, so they have a visual representation to follow.

The great thing about this game is that it doesn't have to be done as a separate computer coding lesson, but can be done as a PE lesson. To make children safe and avoid having them run around and risk bumping into each other, you can tell them they have to move slowly like robots.

Learning Outcomes

This teaches children conditional statements, as you are using the 'IF this happens THEN you do this' language.

It teaches children to listen and follow instructions as well as think logically. If you are giving rules, such as moving to the correct color in as few steps as possible, then they are problem solving and trying to think ahead.

If/Then Animals

You can do this game with any sort of figures or soft toys. I like animals such as small dinosaurs or farm animals, because you can be creative with the actions and they tend to be easy for children to grip, but pretty much anything you have lying around the house can be used.

One person is the 'programmer' and the animals are the 'computers'. I would, again, recommend modeling this game with the adult being the 'programmer' to start with and then swapping over when your child becomes more confident with the game.

For the purpose of this explanation, I'm going to assume we are doing the activity with dinosaurs. Lay them out on the carpet and then the 'programmer' will give instructions, such as "IF I raise my left hand in the air, THEN the blue dinosaur will jump". The child should then pick up the blue dinosaur (or whatever toy or object you have chosen to use) and make it jump. Another direction can be "IF I wave my right hand THEN the red dinosaur will roar". Again, the child should then carry out the action. Do the actions a couple of times and see if the child can carry out the instruction. If they need reminding then do so. If they do the wrong action say, "Uh-oh that's not right, the dinosaur (or whatever the toy is) needs debugging."

When children are confident you can give a few more IF/THEN condition statements and you can swap over and let them make some up.

You may want to make this more interactive. If so, then instead of the animals the child can be the 'computer' and just do the noises and actions themselves. This works really well in a classroom setting where you want to do the activity with larger groups or as a whole class PE session. For example, have the children stand in a space then say something like, "IF I wave my left hand THEN you all jump up and down." You can even assign certain attributes to children, so for example, "IF I wave my left hand THEN everyone who has blond hair has to jump up and down." "IF I wave my right hand THEN everyone wearing shorts has to hop on one leg," and so on.

If/Then Models

Another way of modelling If and Then statements is to make a sculpture using modelling clay or Playdoh. Depending on your child's age and ability you can use 3D or 2D shapes.

Set out conditions such as, "If you roll a two, then you add a rectangle/cuboid."

"If you roll a three then you add a square/cube."

You can write these statements out on paper using dots to symbolize the numbers on the dice.

Roll the die and then follow the statement to make a sculpture or picture.

Learning Outcomes

The learning outcomes are the same as the previous game; it teaches if/then concepts, but it also has an extra mathematical element to it as children are using shapes, so you can use this to consolidate their understanding of 2D or 3D shapes as well.

If you wanted to add in addition, then you can use two dice or even three and they have to add the totals up to see what shape they are adding.

You don't have to do this with Playdoh; you can use building blocks instead.

While and Do

This is similar to the above If and Then but uses While and Do statements instead. At home this can be done outside in the garden or in a room that has space. At school it can be done in a playground, classroom or hall. As it is physical, it can again be used as part of a PE lesson.

The premise of the game is to give an instruction such as "WHILE I do X, you do Y" for instance, WHILE I tap my head, you wave your hands" or "WHILE I count to ten, you jump up and down", "WHILE I clap my hands, you spin around".

The actions can only be completed when the conditions are met, so if you stand and are doing nothing, the children should be doing nothing. If you are patting your head then the children need to be waving, but as soon as you stop they should stop.

Once they have grasped the concept the child/children can then take it in turns to give instructions in this manner.

Learning Outcomes

This is related to the loops we discussed earlier; WHILE a certain condition is met in a game, something will happen. This teaches this basic loop concept, as well as consolidating listening skills and gives children confidence in using this type of language and giving instructions.

Copying Games

Back to Back Copying

These games are great for learning to give step by step directions and learning how to break these down into small steps, as well as showing the importance of giving these steps in a methodical way.

One person gives an instruction and the other one copies. The goal is to replicate something that the person giving the instructions is looking at. This can be a model that they have made out of Lego, wooden blocks, a 2D shape picture or a simple drawing.

This game is best played in pairs. The players sit back to back or have a board between them so they can't see what the other person is doing. The child can make the model or picture first or you can give it to them. Again, this depends on context, age and ability.

Let's say you are playing at home with your child using wooden blocks. You have made a structure. Now you have to describe this to the child for them to replicate so you might say first place a blue cuboid/rectangle on its end, next place a cube/square on top. You can specify color or just use shape.

While it sounds like an easy game, if the person giving the instructions isn't exact, the person following can end up with an entirely different structure.

Learning Objectives

This teaches the importance of giving instructions precisely and in the correct order and demonstrates what happens if something isn't sequenced correctly.

It is a fun game that also consolidates mathematical concepts such as positional language and shape names.

Color on Command

For this game you need a stack of cards with different directions written on them. These can be as simple as arrows.

Give the child some graph paper with large squares or just draw squares on yourself. The bigger the squares the quicker the game will be; the smaller the squares the longer it will last, so this will again be dependent on age. You can draw the squares by hand or do it on the computer.

Let the child choose where to start. This can be a square in the middle of the piece of paper or at an edge or corner. When they have colored it in they pick a card and follow the direction, so if it is an arrow that says forward one then they color the next square along. If it says turn right or left, they choose a square to the right or left of the one they have just colored.

You can add in 'debugging' concepts if they pick a card that then takes them off the edge of the page. Simply say something like, "Uh-oh, there's a bug, we need to re-program the pen by choosing a different card."

If you want to make this more challenging, then you can add in If/Then statements such as "If you choose a card that is forwards THEN you color the square in red". "If you choose a card that says turn THEN you color the square in blue".

Written Codes

Writing and deciphering codes can be great fun and encourage children to think logically to work out a puzzle. These codes can be done on the go as a time filler when you are waiting at a restaurant, for example, or on a larger scale as part of a treasure hunt at home (or in school).

Vowel Codes

CVC words that have a Consonant Vowel Consonant so words such as CAT, CAR, MAT, HAT, PET, POT, CUT and so on are CVC words. Children learn this in their first year of full-time school when they are learning to sound out words phonetically.

This game is a fun one to do just as a five or ten minute filler, as a starter activity in a classroom or even while you are waiting in a doctor's offices or at a restaurant.

Of course, these aren't going to work with preschoolers that can't read; children need to know the concept of CVC words and be able to read them in order to decipher the codes.

To make it simple, start off with just two symbols or stickers to represent two different vowels. For example, A can be a picture of an apple and E can be a picture of an Egg, so the word cat would be C (apple picture) T and the word pet would be P (egg picture) T. If you are using stickers, then you can just use choose a star to represent A, and a circle to represent E, or even different colored stickers so blue circle = A and red circle = E and so on.

Once these have been worked out and the child is familiar with the concept, they can move on to write their own CVC words using a sticker or picture to represent a vowel. In a school setting you can either decipher these as a whole class or children can swap with each other and decipher them by themselves.

The next step is to choose a picture, sticker, or symbol for each of the five vowels. For older children, you can then use a random picture or symbol rather than stickers so # can represent A, * might represent E and so on, and you can write different words and sentences, not just CVC words. For example, if A = *, E = #, I = %, O = $ and U = @: then I L O V E Y O U can be written as:

% L $ V # Y $ @

Treasure Hunt Codes

Firstly choose the 'treasure' you are going to hunt for. At home, this can be treats, like sweets, chocolate coins, small biscuits, or it can just be small toys like cars, wooden animals, beads, or plastic coins. Remember, you can adapt these games to suit your situation. If you want to give your child a treat and want a fairly long treasure hunt, but don't want to give your child large number of sweets, then you can either hide beads or animals and each will have a letter stuck to them. Once collected and put in the correct order, they can spell out where their treat is hidden. You can even hide laminated letters that spell this out. Another idea is that they collect plastic coins and 'pay' for their treat at the end.

You can even hide the codes, so each one leads to a new code which leads to another and then the final prize at the end. This is harder for you, however, as you need to make sure the codes are in the correct order, or at least that the one leading to the treasure is given last.

In a classroom scenario, the idea would be to collect as many coins in an allotted time, working as a team or splitting children into small groups of five and competing so that whichever team collects the most is the winner.

Once you have chosen what you are hiding, you need to write out a code on several different cards. The amount you write depends on how long you want the game to last or how many objects you are hiding. If you have hidden six sweets, for example, then you will need six clues. If you are hiding lots of different objects, then the child/children can decide what order they solve the codes in, which means if they get stuck on one you can encourage them to put it to one side and come back to it rather than just giving up; this teaches them perseverance and patience.

The type of code you use is dependent upon the age and ability of the child/children. An easy one is just replacing letters of the alphabet with numbers and writing where the object is hidden.

For instance, let's pretend for the sake of the example that I am hiding plastic coins, and I have put one in a shoe. I am simply going to write "shoe" in code. My code is using a number for a letter so A = 1, B = 2 and so on therefore my card will read: 19 8 15 5

I would suggest that you write down the code beforehand, so if you are doing the number code you should have a card or piece of paper with the letters of the alphabet on it and then next to or underneath the corresponding number. For younger children, you can then give them this card to help them, so they just have to find the number to see what letter it is and write this down to solve the clue. For older children, you can just let them see if they can decipher it themselves; what ideas can they come up with? This is great for a classroom setting where they can discuss ideas as a group but will still work one on one at home with the child making suggestions or the adult prompting ideas.

Other examples of codes can be swapping the alphabet around, so A = Z and B = Y and so on. In the example above, with this code, the word SHOE would be written as: H S L V

Another idea would be using symbols instead of letters. If you are giving the code card to children, then it can be whatever you want. But if you are trying to get older children to work it out for themselves, then try to make symbols correspond to letters that look or sound similar. For example, you can use @ for A, $ for S, $ for E and so on.

You can make it more complicated and get children to design a code wheel beforehand; there are lots of ideas for these on the Internet. They then use this code wheel to decipher your code. The clever thing about these wheels is that there can be several different codes that can be used. You have one, and the child has one. You set up your code, then they try to decide how you set the wheel up by process of elimination.

For younger children, you can use symbols similar to Makaton symbols. For example, if you were in a classroom and you had hidden treasures in the home corner on the bed, then you can have a picture of a house with the plus symbol and then a picture of a bed.

Again, adapt it to your children's age, ability and interests.

Math Codes

You can add in a bit of mathematics practice while playing these coding games, as well. This can be either as part of a treasure hunt or just written down on paper for the fun of solving them. You can add in an extra challenge by saying, "How many can you solve in three/five/ten minutes?" and setting a timer.

For example, using the numbers instead of a letters code, where A = 1 and B = 2 you can leave spaces or draw a line for each letter and underneath write a math sum. The child works out the sum, which gives them a number, which they then have to translate into a letter.

An example of I LOVE YOU would be

—   ——   ——   ——   ——   ——   ——   ——

3×3 $15-3$ 5×3 11×2 $10-5$ $30-5$ $30-15$ $20-1$

So $3\times3 = 9$, which corresponds to the letter I. $15 - 3 = 12$, which corresponds to the letter L and so on. Of course, these are just examples. Make the sums as easy or difficult as you want depending on the age and ability of the children. For five and six year old's, you may want to use minus and addition sums; for older children who are familiar with multiplication and division, you can start using those.

Learning Outcomes

By working out written codes, children are problem solving and refining their logical thinking skills. There is an element of literacy and mathematics if using number, letter, or symbol codes. They are also working in a methodical way. For example, to decipher your code with a code wheel, they need to try different options until the correct one is apparent.

At home, working with a sibling or an adult or in a classroom situation, children who are working together to solve these puzzles and codes are also using their collaboration and teamwork skills.

Encouraging children to design their own codes helps them be creative.

Creating Functions

It is all well and good teaching children to create algorithms and give instructions, but once they have mastered this technique, saying move forward, move forward, turn right, move forward, move forward, can take forever and is very long winded. Even writing instructions can take longer than necessary if you are drawing three or four arrows in the same direction.

In reality, computers aren't programmed like this and, therefore, teaching functions is helpful once children can follow and give instructions.

You can start this lesson by asking children to come up with their own ways to write down directions like "move forward three spaces". In a classroom setting, this works well, as children can bounce ideas off each other and collaborate, whereas at home, children may need some encouragement, in which case give them some help and make suggestions if they are struggling.

An idea should be something like writing an arrow with a number, so move forward 3 spaces may be denoted as an arrow pointing upwards with the number three before or after it. Right four spaces might be a right arrow with the number four before or after it.

Once they have grasped the idea of writing functions in this way, they can use them as part of one of the maze games, treasure hunts and so on as described above, but this time, instead of speaking commands, they write down the functions. They are written in the correct order so that the other person can then copy them to solve the maze or treasure hunt. Another option is for children to work in pairs or as a group and each person writes down functions (or each pair write down functions) then other people in the group can take turns to follow each other's directions.

I don't recommend this activity for very young children; they have to grasp the idea of giving and following directions before they start to learn about functions. Really, these are aimed at children aged seven and above.

Human Train

This is a game to practice functions but works better in a classroom setting with a lot of children. It can work with one child and one adult but may be more difficult. It needs a large space, so either outside in a back garden, a playground, or in a school hall is ideal.

As it works better with a large number of children, I'm going to assume that you are a class teacher just for explanation purposes.

First, you need to have discussed functions and how to write them, then each child takes a small card, like an index card or a small piece of paper, and writes a direction. This can be an arrow to the right, and a number 8 to show move right eight spaces, or it can be an arrow pointing upwards and a number five to show move forward five spaces. For older children, they can each write two or three on a card. For example one child might write:

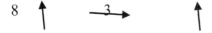

This might mean move forward 8 spaces, turn right, and move forward three spaces.

Once they have all finished, take the cards from the children and shuffle them. Then ask them to line up in single file. You can ask them to stand with their hands on the shoulders of the child in front of them, but this is optional.

Tell the children they are a train, and they each have to follow the person in front of them and stay in single file. You are going to 'program' them to move. Stand at the front of the line and hold up the first card, and read aloud the instructions. The children all have to move the way they have been told, so in the above example, they would move forward eight steps, turn to the right and move forward three steps. Continue until every card has been read aloud. If a child (or children) move the wrong way, tell them the train needs 'debugging' and give them a chance to work out where they went wrong as a group.

You can also turn this into a competition by having two or three lines and seeing which group can follow the directions correctly, or have children read out the instructions. You can even have five children, each holding a card up, and five other children being the 'train' and following the directions all in one go.

This game would still works one on one at home, but you would need to write quite a few different directions in order for it to last, and these would then need to be read out loud by the person in front if you wanted to be a train, otherwise, you can have it as robot and programmer instead.

Hopscotch Functions

I am assuming everybody is familiar with the game Hopscotch. Draw a grid (usually one square, then two side by side, then one above in the middle again, and so on) and write numbers in each square.

This coding game uses the same style grid drawn outside with chalk, but instead of throwing a stone and hopping in the same set pattern, the 'programmers' choose the pattern.

Instead of numbers, draw the grid but write a symbol in each square. The 'programmer' then writes down different symbols for the 'robot' or 'computer' to land on. For example, say you have a #, a % sign, and a $ sign in your grid. You might write something like 3#, 2$, 4%, which can mean hop three times on the # square, jump to the $ square and hop twice, jump to the % square and hop four times.

Learning Outcomes

For all the above games, the learning outcomes are understanding and being able to write functions as well as giving and following instructions written using functions and code.

It also teaches listening skills as well as patience and perseverance if they make a mistake.

If children are working together, it again hones their collaboration skills.

Chapter Four

Coding Resources on the Market

There are plenty of coding resources available to purchase online or in stores that are specifically aimed at teaching children coding concepts. In fact, the predictions for the 'must have' Christmas toys have several coding resources in the list this year.

I don't necessarily recommend one over the other. Like anything, they all have pros and cons and whichever you choose – if any - will depend on your child's preferred learning style, your budget and possibly how much space you have in your home or how long you think you will spend playing with the item. I would always recommend checking the reviews on products before purchasing, as these can often be a good indicator of how good the toy is and whether it is suitable or not.

Books

There are plenty of coding books out there directed at children who want to learn to code. These range from the simple, toddler board books, through to lift the flap and storybooks right up to informational text that guide you through the steps to make your own computer game.

You can purchase generic "what is coding and where is it used in everyday life" type books, or more specific ones that are tailored towards learning an actual programming language, such as Scratch or Python.

These books are great, but of course, if you are trying to follow one that teaches a programming language and shows you how to make a computer game, then you are going to need to have a computer or tablet, as well as the relevant software in order to follow it. Therefore, before you purchase the book, I would advise you check whether you can get the software easily and make sure it's compatible for the device your child will be using.

The thing I like about books is that you – or your child – can follow them at your own pace. When they're geared towards children, they tend to be simple text and brightly colored pictures and broken down into simple steps, especially the ones dealing with Scratch and Python. As a parent or teacher, if you don't consider yourself technologically minded or you are not as confident with coding, then you can also follow along with these books easily, either working alongside the child or children you are teaching or familiarizing yourself with them before teaching the concepts.

If your child doesn't show much of an interest in factual books, they may respond better to a story style type book. These can still give relevant coding information but in a friendlier, less academic way. Some of these fictional story style books may also include coding activities for your child to do along the way, such as cracking codes.

If you have a daughter, you may find that some of these books specifically target girls and have a strong female main character because there is a big push at the moment to encourage girls to follow a career in STEM subjects.

Board Games

There are now board games that are directly related to coding concepts and have been designed with this in mind. Many started out as Kickstarter projects. Usually, they will have code cards, which players have to set out in a specific order which will get their counter or character to some sort of reward. For instance, Robot Turtles requires players to move their turtle around the board in order to collect a jewel. If someone makes a mistake, they can 'debug' and undo one of their moves. Some of these games can be made more complex by adding extra cards and directions.

Many of these games are played out until everyone has successfully directed their counter to the correct squares. So everyone is a winner, which encourages teamwork, as once one person has successfully 'programmed and won' they can help other people.

While I like the concept of these games, I think a lot of them are similar to the maze games described above, so you can in fact make your own version of them. However, what I like about them is that sometimes you can interest a child more with a new game than with an activity you have set up yourself. It also means there is very limited preparation needed because everything is in the box and it means you can get it out whenever you want without having to search for resources. It is also a great way to involve the whole family without feeling like a 'lesson' and can be a great gift for birthdays or Christmas.

Robots

Now we are getting to the more high tech, and therefore, more expensive end of the coding toy spectrum.

There is a large variety of programmable coding 'bots' about now, which vary from the small, cheap ones right up to the larger, more complex ones. Of course, the more you pay, the more your robot will do, and the more your child can code and interact with them, but that doesn't always mean they are the best. When choosing a robot, I would look at reviews and also your child's ability. Is a five year old who is just learning basic concepts going to have the patience to sit and code a robot that is complex?

At the low end of the price range, you have the type that you just push a few buttons to adjust the direction of the robot in order to program it to go from one place to another. Usually, they just have right, left, forward and back, although there are some that have pieces that the child can pull apart and click into place in a certain order to make it move. Some of these come with a maze, whereas others are just meant to play on the floor, and your child can program it and predict where it is going to end up. These basic ones, like the Bee Bots, are the type you tend to see in nurseries and schools and are great for younger children to get to grips with programming instructions to get it to move in a certain way.

For older children, these will be a bit too simplistic and they may tire of them quickly, although you can make it more interesting by getting them to make their own mazes for it to run through or getting them to write the directions first and then program it, trying to predict where it will end up, which will extend their learning.

On the more expensive end of the price range, there are miniature robots that can hiccup, recognize familiar faces, play music and even challenge your child to compete with them in memory games. You can get robots that dance or can be programmed to move in a certain way. Some of them will have upgrades that can be unlocked when a certain criteria has been met, which makes them interesting and can encourage your child to play with them more in order to unlock more features.

I think the robots are great, however, one drawback with the expensive ones is that they often need a tablet or smartphone in order to work. If you are trying to reduce the amount of screen time your child has, then this probably isn't the way to do it. However, for older children that are ready to learn to code using a computer, these can be a great resource.

As with anything, you get what you pay for. If you want a robot that is all singing, all dancing (literally) and which your child programs with lots of chances for coding, then this is going to cost you, but is it worth it? This is where checking the reviews is advisable and knowing whether your child is going to lose interest quickly or not.

Build Your Own Computer

When I was a child, computers didn't really exist in the domestic household, so the concept of actually building one would have been completely alien to me. Nowadays, kits can be bought so that children as young as six can build their own computer (with parental help) and then complete certain coding challenges, which gives them hands on experience in how computers actually work.

Clearly this is moving beyond the basic concepts we were talking about when we look at offline coding, but it is an amazing resource if you can afford it, as it allows children hands on experience.

These kits are expensive, and I wouldn't recommend purchasing one unless your child is really into coding or loves taking toys apart and building them again. However, it is a wonderful challenge and would be a great learning experience. I think they are also a great activity for children and parents to do together.

Chapter Five

Coding Online

So your child has done lots of offline coding activities and have enjoyed them, but how do you get them coding using an actual computer?

This is going to be difficult to explain in a book such as this without having pages and pages of diagrams and jargon and to be fair there are lots of books dedicated to teaching children Scratch and Python that I don't think it's needed to go into depth and do a step by step instruction. There are also many amazing websites and apps out there that can be downloaded, so this chapter is going to look at the best ones to use with children when they are first learning to code as well as ones that are suitable for more able or older coders.

Many websites and apps will promise that your child can learn to build their own apps and computer games, which sounds amazing, but just beware that this isn't going to happen within a few hours. They are not going to sit down at the computer and suddenly build a fantastic computer game using code. However, if they sit and learn step by step they will eventually learn the skills to do this; so let's look at the best places to start.

Coding Blocks Or Text-Based Coding?

When you think of coding and programming languages you may instantly imagine long lines of nonsense letters, numbers and symbols strung together that are meaningless to a non-technical minded human being yet that isn't the case nowadays; yes some computer languages are like that but for young children just starting out they can learn to build computer games and apps in a colorful virtual world with fun characters using nothing more than coding blocks that are linked together to build instructions.

Visual block coding, while it seems simple, allows children to practice concepts like the if/then conditional statements and allows them to build their own game without spending hours poring over the keyboard to find the right key.

These drag and drop blocks are a simple stepping-stone into coding. They are not meant to be used forever. The idea is that young children as young as five can start coding using a computer, tablet or smartphone, or whatever, will gain an interest and then move on to other, more complicated programming languages.

Text-based coding, on the other hand, tends to use actual programming languages. This can seem more complicated (and it is), but if you choose a platform that is aimed at children such as Coda Kid, then children as young as eight years old can actually use these languages and have fun doing so.

There is no right or wrong answer, so whichever you choose will be dependent on your child (or children), how much you want to spend on resources and the type of hardware you are using.

For younger children, aged 5-8 years, then block-based is easier to teach and can give children a bit more independence, as once they have mastered the basics can start to work by themselves. In a classroom setting, this may be preferable as you can teach the whole class how to do a certain task and then let them explore by themselves in pairs, and you are then free to move around each one, helping or challenging them where necessary. It can reduce frustration for those children who maybe aren't into computer programming and coding or don't understand it and are worried about it being difficult.

For a parent or teacher who doesn't consider themselves a 'techie' then block-based coding is also good for you to learn because you can pick it up fairly quickly.

However, that said, I can see the value of jumping straight into giving a child the experience of real life software creation by using more advanced computer languages, especially if you are working in a school that has a certain subscription in place already. It is easier for children to see how it can apply to their future endeavors, and there is nothing wrong with doing this as long as it is taught in a fun, child-friendly way, otherwise, it can put them off if they find it long-winded and boring.

Online Resources

Hour of Code

This is a global initiative in over 180+ countries and began as a way of introducing computer science in order to make coding less mysterious and prove that really anybody can learn the basics.

The Hour of Code takes place every year during Computer Science Education week. This is a global event, however, the tutorials stay up all year round, so you don't have to participate in an event to use these at home or at school. You can even set your own event up if you wish to do so.

The reason I mention it here is because the actual concept of 'an hour of coding' is great; if you don't want your child to have a lot of computer screen time, but they are ready to move on to coding with a computer, then an hour is long enough for them to learn without getting too frustrated or spending too long sat in front of a screen or on a tablet.

Scratch

There are other websites and apps that are now starting to use drag and drop, block-based coding, however, this is the original one. It allows children to create basic games in a colorful, virtual world with fun characters known as 'Sprites'.

Scratch is popular because it is fun, simple to use and best of all it is free! Therefore in a home or school setting I think it is worth playing about with it yourself to see if you like it and then introducing it to your child.

If you are a teacher in a classroom setting, then playing about beforehand means you can build your lesson plans based on what you have learned.

If you are a parent, then it is fun for you to have a grasp on how it works just in case your child gets stuck. I would recommend that you work side by side with them and make it a fun activity rather than a structured learning experience and just let them play about and learn at their own pace.

For those that don't feel confident with computers or who have tried Scratch and don't understand it, there are lots of good books and resources out there that explain it in a simple, step by step way so it might be worth buying one of these and following along so that your child does learn in a structured way rather than playing about, not understanding it and giving up because they don't have an aim.

Some people are negative about Scratch and other block-based coding, saying it is not real programming, however, it is only meant to be an introduction to coding and computer programming. Once children have mastered Scratch, then move on.

Subscriptions

Tynker

Tynker's tagline is "coding made easy" and it delivers this via award-winning block and text based courses, learning modules, and daily coding missions aimed at different ages and abilities. It offers a limited number of iPhone and iPad courses.

For example, children 4-7 years old can use voice instruction to learn the basics of coding, solve logic problems, and create simple apps.

Children 7-13 years can use drag and drop code blocks to build apps and games, as well as exploring STEM subjects. They can control robots and drones and even design their own Minecraft Mods.

For those aged 13+, JavaScript, and Python, courses are available, as well as web design using HTML and CSS.

The great thing about Tykner is that children can learn at their own pace; if they master one section they can move onto the next. There is also a monthly skill assessment so you, as an adult, as well as your child, can see how much they've accomplished.

The downside is that it is a subscription-based website, and you can pay either a monthly subscription, which starts at $10, a quarterly subscription, which start from $20 or a lifetime subscription, which starts at $240. (Prices were correct at the time of this book going to print and are dependent on whether you choose an individual or family plan).

There are a few free modules that all you to 'try before you buy' and it is worth doing this to get a feel for whether you like it or not. While it is similar to Scratch, there is more direction and pathways and is geared towards older children who have more coding experience as well as just young children wanting basic knowledge.

As there are so many courses available and it covers many age groups and abilities, it does make it an excellent resource to use in a classroom setting if your school is willing to pay the subscription fees.

Bitsbox

This is a monthly subscription box and contains coding challenges that use Java script. It is around $25 per month for a physical box, or you can get the digital version for around $17 per month.

Aimed at 6-12 year olds, no prior coding experience is necessary. Children learn to build games and apps, which can then be played by themselves and others in the family.

Coda kid

This is a great website because it contains free blogs for parents and teachers who may not be as technically minded as their child/children, so you can be reassured that they can learn alongside their child. There are lots of video tutorials as well as mentor support.

Subscriptions start at around $25 per month and around $249 for a year.

Unlike Tynker or Scratch, however, it is aimed at older kids between 8-15 years, so may not be the best place to start for those who are just beginning their coding journey.

The following are more suitable for teenagers and young adults, aged 16 year upwards.

Codeacademy

This is a mixture of free and paid for online courses, so it might be worth trying a couple of free ones before jumping in to pay the subscription fee, which starts at around $17.99 a month. The pro level, paid for courses, includes portfolio building projects and quizzes. So if your teen is a future computer programmer in the making, it might be ideal for them to gain experience in this field.

Treehouse

This is an online coding school, which provides vocational training for those who have an interest in full-stack development, data science, and web development. Subscriptions start at around $25 per month.

Udemy

This has lots of videos and coding tutorials on game development, machine learning, web development, full-stack development, and so on. Prices start from around $11,99 per course. It is expensive but is aimed at those who are looking to start a career in computer programming.

IPad Apps

The following are free apps available on the iPad.

Daisy the Dinosaur

This is aimed at children as young as four. It teaches basic coding concepts, and once the game is completed there is a downloadable kit that children can use to make their own game.

Hopscotch

Suitable for older children, aged 9-11 years, and this app uses video tutorials that help children build their own video games and allows them to play each other's.

Move the Turtle

This is another free iPad app aimed at children 9-11 years old. It teaches critical thinking, which is beneficial to them, both on and off the computer.

There are plenty of others, but these are the most popular at the moment.

Chapter Six

Patterning and Binary

There is a lot of contention around as to whether to teach children Binary or not. Some argue that young children don't need to learn it as it can be complicated and many computer programmers get along fine only knowing the basics of binary. Many people start to learn it as part of a computer programming course only at college or university level.

While all this may be true, I think that teaching children patterning is a basic mathematical concept, and therefore, once your children has grasped the concept of patterns and you are teaching them coding, then a knowledge of basic binary puts them ahead of their peers. Even if they don't want to be a computer programmer when they are older, and never use this knowledge, it doesn't harm to learn something new, plus there are lots of fun activities.

As this is a book aimed at teaching coding to children, as with the offline coding games, I am only looking at activities that teach children patterns and binary at a basic level as opposed to trying to get them ready for a university degree.

Patterning

Before jumping straight into teaching your child binary, they need to understand the concept of patterns. These can start basic for preschoolers and work up to the more complex.

Clapping and Stamping Patterns

Very young children love copying and a child as young as two can do a basic clapping pattern just by copying you, and it is a fun game to play.

With young children, tell them to copy you. Do two claps then see if they do the same. Next, stomp your feet twice and get them to copy. When they have done this, then do a clap, stomp, clap, stomp, clap, stomp and see if they can join in with you. This is the pattern; one clap followed by one stamp.

Once they have grasped this pattern try another one: two claps, two stamps or one clap, two stamps. Repeat until they have picked up the pattern.

A two-year-old will just copy you - they won't grasp the concept of a pattern as such, but a four year old should start to notice the repetition. Call their attention to this by saying out loud what you are doing. Next, ask them if they can follow the pattern, for example, if it is one clap, one stamp, one clap one stamp, do this several times saying aloud "clap, stamp, clap, stamp, clap, stamp, clap..."

After the last clap, ask them what comes next? If they can answer either verbally or by doing the action praise them and do another pattern.

Once they can identify each pattern, ask them to do their own for you to copy.

For older children who already understand the concept of patterns, you can do more complicated ones such as two claps, two stamps, pat your head, two claps, and two stamps, pat your head, and so on. Add in three or four or more actions depending on the child's age and ability.

In a classroom setting, this is a great PE warm up, but you can also make it a specific coding activity by demonstrating patterns in the above way and then putting children in groups of four or five. Can they come up with a pattern with each of them doing an action, and can other children then join in? For example, a pattern can be two claps, one stamp, two jumps, and one hop. The children will stand in a line, and one child will do two claps. The next will stamp once. The third will then jump twice and the fourth child will hop then they would repeat. You can ask the children who are watching to jump in when they have identified the pattern so for example, when someone has picked up the pattern they can join the end of the line and do the two claps, someone else would join them and do the one stamp, continue until everybody is in the line. Can they keep the pattern going?

Bead Patterns

All you need for this activity are colored beads and string or pipe cleaners to thread them on. For young children, you will need to demonstrate. Simply thread a bead onto the string or pipe cleaner, then another one. Start with a simple pattern with two colors, such as red, blue, red, blue, red blue. When your child can identify the pattern, then do another one. Once they understand the concept then they can make their own. Progress on to three color patterns such as green, blue, yellow, green, blue, yellow, and then more complicated ones such as red, red, green, blue, red, red, green, blue, and so on.

For older children, you can use more colors and more complicated patterns. You can even use different shaped beads instead of (or as well as) colors so the pattern might be red heart, yellow star, yellow star, and blue cube.

Peg Board Patterns

If you have a simple peg board, then children can do lots of different patterns with these. For instance, they can go around the outside edge in one color, then move in a row and go around again in a different color, then go around again in the first color, moving inwards towards the middle.

Another pattern can be doing a row in blue, followed by a row in red, followed by two rows of green and a row of blue again.

Again, they can be as simple or as complicated as the child can think of as long as they are repeating patterns and not just random colors.

Shape Patterns

Patterns don't have to be just colors; they can be shapes. Children can cut out their own shapes from cards or colored paper or use pre-cut ones and glue them on a large piece of paper in a pattern such as square, rectangle and square rectangle. You can even use stamps if you didn't want to glue and stick.

Musical Sound Patterns

Why not make sound patterns with musical instruments such as quiet and loud or bells then drums. You can do this as a circle activity with children continuing the pattern around the circle, for example, one child plays their instrument quietly, the next plays loud, the next play quiet. For young children around four or five years of age, you can explain this as a whole group and tell them what the pattern is and then once they have grasped the concept ask the children to come up with different patterns themselves.

For older or more able children, you can explain the game of continuing the sound pattern around the circle, but then you can take three or four children to one side and explain the pattern. These children join the circle and you and they start the pattern off, like the clap/stamp pattern game explained above, when the other children think they know they pattern they can join in or carry it on until it goes around the circle. Repeat again with a different pattern. You

70

can even let children pick their pattern, and then they perform it, and the adults see if they can guess it.

Number Patterns

Okay, as coding has its roots in mathematics and computer science, we had to get onto number concepts sooner or later, didn't we? But who says that numbers and math can't be made fun? I love number patterns because I think it can be fun and teach children to think analytically, looking for what is the same and what is different about each line. It's kind of like looking at code and spotting the pattern is like debugging if you have a question mark where a number should be.

Children are learning number patterns all the time when they are learning to count and when they're counting in two's, five's, etc. or learning prime numbers.

Examples of number patterns include:

3... 5... 7... 9... 11... What comes next? Can children spot that these are all odd numbers and go up by two each time?

What about the pattern 30... 25... 20... 15... Can children spot the numbers decrease by five each time?

1... 2... 4... 7... 11... 16... Can children spot that each number goes up by one, then two, then three, then four, then five? Can they carry on the pattern?

What about 1... 2... 4... 8... 16... 32... Do children spot that it's doubling the number? Also known as to the power of 2, which is something we'll come to when we look at binary, so these numbers will shortly become very important.

You can give children these number patterns as work sheets, or you can do them as a group using an interactive whiteboard or number lines, or you can make them more interactive. A nice carpet activity is for children to have whiteboards and pens and you write a number on two or three and get these children to hold the boards up and stand in a line and the other children to guess what the next number is, write it on their whiteboard and join the line. You can put confident learners in two or three teams and see which team comes up with the answer first, awarding points in a game show style contest.

Pretty much any resource can be made into patterns. You can use potato printing and make different color patterns – or use different vegetables to make different shape patterns.

Using natural resources outdoors, you can make patterns such as twig, leaf, stone, twig, leaf, and stone.

You can use sticks to draw repeating patterns in the sand tray or why not try cutting out play dough and laying it in shapes?

If you're baking cookies, you can cut out two or three different shapes and lay them out in patterns on the baking tray.

You can make size patterns with different items like teddy bears or toys such as big, small, medium, big, small, medium.

Really, your only limit is your imagination.

Binary

As I mentioned above, it is a bit of a contentious point about whether you should or shouldn't teach binary to children. I'm not going to argue the pros and cons; the reason I like it and add it here is because it is a computer concept related to coding. It's another type of pattern, and mostly I'm writing about it because it is fun! Whether children use it or not in any other context, then who cares as long as they enjoy learning it? If nothing else, it can help their math skills.

As with all these games and activities, it isn't just about learning binary so they can program a computer, but at this stage, it is just about learning different concepts and having fun. Again it can also teach children to be logical and analytical thinkers, which is a valuable skill to have just in life in general.

Now I'm not saying teach a four-year-old binary. This would be way too difficult for a child that is really just grasping how to count in single digits and learning how to add and minus without adding binary on top. Really these activities are aimed at children around eight or nine who have a good grasp of basic mathematical number concepts and can recognize fairly complex number patterns.

As an adult, binary can be fairly complex and may take a while to get your head around it if you have never come across it before, so I advise you try to pick it up and have a basic understanding of it yourself before you try to teach your child or class.

If, after this chapter, you are still not sure about how to work out 5-bit binary codes, then Google YouTube videos that are geared directly for children, as these may help you grasp the concept a little bit easier.

In fact, you may not really be aware of what binary is, so here is a mini explanation of what it is and how it relates to computers and coding.

What Is Binary?

Usually, when we count we use the decimal system, which consists of 10 digits: 0-9. Binary, however, only consists of two digits: 0 and 1.

Computers use binary as a way of storing data because it is reliable. Sounds, graphics, colors, words; everything a computer stores and displays is all converted into binary.

Of course, this is a simple explanation, and it is rather more complex, but for children who are just learning binary code and coding, this is enough to know.

Now, if a binary code is used for a number and for letters, then a string of binary by itself doesn't have any meaning because how do we know if the binary string we see stands for a number or a letter? Just like listening to phonic sounds when reading, the binary string needs some context around it in order to know what you are seeing. This is where binary gets complicated, but for the purpose of teaching basic binary, it is wise to start with numbers and then move on to letters, letting children know when they are decoding words and when they are decoding numbers.

All children really need to know is that computers store information in binary and that this number system only uses two digits.

Letters are usually interpreted by computers using UTF-8, which is eight digit binary. Each character is assigned an eight digit binary string, but for the purpose of teaching children binary, to start with it is easier to use 5 string binary codes, and this is what the focus of this chapter will be on. You can move on to longer strings when the children have grasped the 5-bit binary concept.

Teaching Binary

First, a 'Bit' means Binary Digit. A five string 'bit', therefore, uses 5 digits that are all either 0 or 1.

In the decimal number system, we always use 10 digits as explained above. These are: 0, 1, 2, 3, 4, 5, 6, 7, 8, 9. When we get to nine, to move to the next number, we move the one into the tens place and put a zero into the ones place, which makes the number 10. Likewise, when we get to 99, in order to write the number 100, we simply put a one in the hundreds place, a zero in the tens place and a

The number 17 then would be 10001 as the first one is in the sixteens place and the last one is at the end so stands for one. 16 + 1 = 17.

Hand Activity

A good visual for children (and often adults) can be using our fingers to count. Get the children to draw around their left hand and then write the above numbers on each finger, so 1 would be written on the thumb, 2 would be written on the index finger, 4 is written on the middle finger, 8 is on the fourth finger, and 16 is on the little finger.

This hand diagram can now be placed in front of them. Now ask the children (or child if you are doing this at home) to lift their right hand up. Curl all their fingers up so none of them are held up. This equals zero. Explain to the children that whenever a finger is held down, this stands for zero.

Next, ask the children to hold up their thumb only. All the other fingers are down. What number are they holding up in binary? Get the children to look down at their hand diagram; one is written on the thumb; therefore, they are holding up one.

Repeat, but this time with the index finger; this is number two.

Repeat again with each finger held up by itself. Get the children to do a quick recap to show they understand by telling them to show… and then pick a number, so, for example, "show 8" they should hold up only their fourth finger and curl down the others. "Show 16"; they should curl up all fingers and just hold up their smallest finger.

Once they have grasped this concept, ask them if they can show the number three in binary using their fingers. This should be the thumb and the index finger (2 + 1 = 3).

Next, can they show 5. (Middle finger is four so they should hold up the middle finger and the thumb – 4 + 1 = 5).

Work out different sums adding up the digits on their fingers.

Ask children if they can work out what number is shown in binary if all their fingers are held up? (This is a simple addition $16 + 8 + 4 + 2 + 1 = 31$).

Work as a whole class group in a school setting or as homework together with your child until they have grasped the concept of adding up the different numbers.

Show them how you write this down in binary. For example, let's say they wanted to show the number 19 in binary. They need to work out which numbers add up to this and hold these fingers up. This would be their smallest finger (16), their index finger (2) and their thumb (1).

Remember the fingers that are held down stand for zeros so the easiest way to work it out would be to write out the five numbers that are written on their hand diagram then underneath put a 1 for the fingers they are holding up and a zero for the fingers they are holding down so they should have something like this:

16 8 4 2 1

1 0 0 1 1

Children may need quite a bit of support before they grasp this concept.

Once they start to show an understanding, you can write down some numbers and ask them to convert it to binary, so if you wrote down the number 24, for example, they would have to look at the five numbers on their hand diagram and see which ones added up to 24 (16 and 8). They should then be able to write ones for these two numbers and zeros for the next three digits, so therefore the number 24 in binary is 11000.

If you are in a school setting, then let children work in pairs to convert some decimal numbers into binary. If you are at home, then sit and work together with your child.

Once they have done several of these, they can pick their own numbers to convert.

Remember, the highest number they can have is 31, but you can pose this as a challenge question; for example, ask something like, "What is the highest number we can convert into binary using 5- bit strings?"

The answer is 31 because $16 + 8 + 4 + 2 + 1 = 31$.

It will help if children have pen and paper or a small whiteboard and dry wipe pen so they can write down their addition sums to work it out if necessary. This also helps you to see their workings out so you can see if they understand the concept or not.

It may take a lot of practice, but once they have grasped the concept, you can ask them to teach someone else the five digit binary. In a classroom setting you can challenge children to take home their hand diagram and teach a parent or sibling. If you are teaching from home you can challenge them to teach another grown up or a friend.

Once they are used to converting digits to binary, you can move on to converting this to letters. It is similar to the codes we discussed previously, where you can use a number to stand in for a letter, so A would be 1, B would be 2, and so on. If children are used to this type of code, then this makes this activity a bit easier. The only difference is that each letter will not only have a decimal number but a five digit binary string.

Together write down the numbers one to twenty-six and then write the corresponding alphabet letter next to it. Next, ask them if they can use their hand diagram to work out the binary code for each one.

Give them paper and pen to write their workings out on and if they need to write down each addition sum.

In a classroom setting, work in pairs and go around the class helping as necessary. In a home setting, then work with your child, allowing them to work it out but helping whenever they need help.

You can ask them if they can spot any patterns in the binary numbers as they are working their way through the alphabet.

For easy reference the alphabet would be:

1	A	00001
2	B	00010
3	C	00011
4	D	00100
5	E	00101
6	F	00110
7	G	00111
8	H	01000
9	I	01001
10	J	01010
11	K	01011
12	L	01100
13	M	01101
14	N	01110

15	O	01111
16	P	10000
17	Q	10001
18	R	10010
19	S	10011
20	T	10100
21	U	10101
22	V	10110
23	W	10111
24	X	11000
25	Y	11001
26	Z	11010

If in a classroom setting, once everyone has finished, then come back together as a whole class and go through the answers, showing the correct key on the whiteboard and allowing children to compare their answers.

If children make mistakes, embrace this and praise them for trying and work out the correct answer together as a whole class, showing how problems are solved.

If you are working one on one with your child at home, then have the binary alphabet pre-written on a piece of paper or card to compare and let your child see if they are correct. If they are wrong, can they spot their mistakes and work together with you to correct these?

Whether in the classroom setting or at home, always try to foster a good attitude for learning. It is okay to make mistakes because we can learn from them. Have everyone in the classroom be positive and help each other. At home, help your child come to the right answer rather than just giving it to them, or make them work it out for themselves. If you just leave them to it they will get more and more frustrated, but if you work together and have a positive attitude, they will feel less like they are being tested and more like they are just playing a game and having fun.

For the next set of activities, you can either let children work from the alphabet sheet they have created, or you can have pre-made ones; those made from card or that are laminated will last longer than paper ones.

Binary Beads

For this activity, you need some beads and something to thread them on. You can use thin wire, pipe cleaners, string, or whatever you prefer (as mentioned previously). Make sure whatever you choose is small enough to fit through the hole in the beads, so you don't want anything too small, but if you have beads that are too chunky, you run the risk of having a huge end product.

The aim of the activity is for children to either write their birth date (if you want a shorter activity using numbers) or their name (if you want a longer activity using letters).

The upside of doing a birthday is that everyone will use the same format of the XX/XX/XXXX, and everyone will use the same number of beads and therefore have the same sized end product.

Spelling out their name is a longer activity, but means that in a classroom setting some children will have longer names than others.

You may decide based on ability. Those that have grasped the binary concept really well will be capable of doing their name quicker than those who haven't really understood it.

At home, it purely depends on whether you want a longer activity or a shorter one. You can always do one of each on separate days if your child enjoys the activity.

Firstly, get the child (or children) to write down their birthday or name in 5-bit binary code.

For example, the name Sophie would be:

S	O	P	H	I	E
10011	01111	10000	01000	01001	00101

Next, each child needs to pick out three colors: one to show the ones, one to show zeros, and one for spaces between each binary code.

Once they've selected their beads, they just need to thread them together to make a bracelet or necklace, putting a bead to show a space between each 'letter' code.

Crack the Code

Another fun game is to write different words or short phrases in binary code; can children work out what each letter is and solve the code? This is a fun way to do a treasure hunt as you can write a clue in binary code, and they need to solve it to find the next clue, or you can just write little notes to each other, or in a classroom setting, they can write notes to their friends in binary.

Graph Paper Patterns

This involves using graph paper (you can easily print off some from the internet if you don't have any to hand) and writing numbers along the side to show which square children should color in. I think an easy one to start with is to write the five numbers that you used on their hand patterns (16, 8, 4, 2, 1) along the top and then write decimal numbers or binary along the sides; they have to convert the numbers in order to find out which square to color. Once finished, the squares should make a pattern or picture.

You can look online and find some pre-made printable pattern graphs, just make sure if you are teaching 5-bit binary that these printable ones correspond to this as some use 8-bit binary strings.

Sticker Codes

Using those circle dots that you can buy, let children choose two different colors and make their own binary codes; one color stands for 0, and one color stands for 1. They can either write their name or write words or they can just make decimal numbers, whatever task you set them.

Binary Bunting

This is a great one for children to display in their bedrooms. On a separate piece of card, children write each letter of their name in binary – they can also write the corresponding alphabet letter in the center and the binary code underneath if they wish to do so. When finished, they string up each piece of card either lengthways to make bunting or vertically to make a wall hanging. The advantage of this activity is that because it can be hung up on the wall, it doesn't matter how large it is and is a great way to display their work.

Other Activities

There are lots of different resources you can use to make binary codes; for instance, if you have circular and long shaped pasta, children can use this to write their names or make different binary codes.

Outside you can use twigs and stones where twigs stand for 1 and stones stand for zero.

Using play dough, children can use two different colors to represent zero and one and make their binary strings by making play dough balls. You can even have pre-made laminated cards with either the binary codes for each letter or short words, and children can just match their play dough up to these codes shown on the card. So, you may have the letter A and then the binary code underneath but using colored circles to stand for the zeros and ones. If children don't like play dough, you can cut up pool noodles to do the same activity.

If it's coming up to a special holiday, why not make cards with binary letters on saying things like 'happy holidays' or 'Merry Christmas'?

Helping Your Kids Learn Python

It really doesn't matter if you are a parent or teacher; it is quite simple to teach kids how to get started in learning the Python programming language. To finish this book off, we are going to look at some very easy Python tutorials that kids can easily follow. This will give them a great grounding in Python programming, and we'll be focusing on basic programming commands that teach kids the way that Python works and using those commands to develop some fun projects.

I have split this tutorial down into three separate ones, each looking at basic code concepts and how to apply that learned knowledge. Please, don't feel you have to go through these all at once or at breakneck speed. Take them one at a time and run through them at your child's pace – it is important that they understand each concept – what it means, how it works, and how it is used in a program.

Chapter Seven

Tutorial One – Python Syntax, Variables, and Loops

Concepts Covered in This Chapter

In the first tutorial, will be exploring the follow code concepts:

- **Python Syntax** – this is nothing more than the grammar of any computer coding language. In the same way that an English sentence is not easy to understand if the correct grammar and spelling are not used, a computer cannot understand the commands given to it if they are not laid out correctly. Syntax is used to define the correct way of laying computer programming language commands.

- **Variables** – as far as computer programming goes, variables are values that may change. Here, we will look at how variables may be changed and the effect this will have on our program output.

- **Loops** – a Python loop has got some instructions in it; these instructions are repeated over and over until a specified condition has been met. We will be looking at the 'for loop' and the 'while loop', two commonly used loops, and the difference between them.

Installing and Opening Python

If you have not yet installed Python your computer, you should look at a version called Anaconda. It also includes its own IDE, or Integrated Development Environment, called Spyder – this makes programming in Python very easy. It can be downloaded for free from https://conda.io/docs/user-guide/install/inex.html.

An easier way, if you do not want to install Python on your computer just yet, you can use a web-based Python IDE. This will allow you to code in Python, learn any mistakes made and get to grips with the language before you decide if you want to take your learning further. The best one to use is https://repl.it/languages/python3 - open it on your computer and start coding right away!

Time to dive into our first tutorial:

Let's Create a FOR loop

Our first topics will be for loops and variables; let's learn what they are and understand how they work using a command called range.

When you have opened your Python editor – either Spyder or the online interpreter – type in this piece of code – note that the code is indented; this must be followed exactly, or the code will not work:

```
for x in range(1,7):

    print (x)
```

Run this code, making sure you have kept the indent on line two

You should now see this on your screen:

```
1

2

3
```

4

5

6

>>>

What has just happened here? We asked the computer to print the numbers between 1 and 6 – note that it did not print the final number (the range method will not include the last number in the range).

Now change the numbers inside the range() method – method is another name for command. Try changing the numbers and see what happens. With practice, you will come to understand how a list of numbers is constructed in Python inside a specified range.

The goal here is to understand the range() method, the limitations it has – it doesn't print the final number in the range, i.e. 6, in our example – and to learn what variables are.

What else have we done here?

We also made a for loop. What is one of those? As mentioned before a loop is common in computer programs. They provide the computer with some instructions that it must repeat continually until a condition is met. In the for loop, our computer will execute, or run, our command for the however many times we specified in the command – in this case, the range() command specifies this.

We could also ask the computer to show our numbers in the reverse order. To do that, copy the following code into the editor, not forgetting that indentation again:

```
for x in range(7,1,-1):

    print (x)
```

Did you spot what happened? Now this can be used for coding a kid's song using this method so, in the code editor, type in this text:

```
for x in range(5,0,-1):

 print (x, 'funny piglets bouncing on the bed, 1 bounced off and
banged his head, daddy rang the doctor and the doctor said, no more
piglets bouncing on the bed')
```

You should this on your screen:

5 funny piglets bouncing on the bed, 1 bounced off and banged his head, daddy rang the doctor and the doctor said, no more piglets bouncing on the bed

4 funny piglets bouncing on the bed, 1 bounced off and banged his head, daddy rang the doctor and the doctor said, no more piglets bouncing on the bed

3 funny piglets bouncing on the bed, 1 bounced off and banged his head, daddy rang the doctor and the doctor said, no more piglets bouncing on the bed

2 funny piglets bouncing on the bed, 1 bounced off and banged his head, daddy rang the doctor and the doctor said, no more piglets bouncing on the bed

1 funny piglets bouncing on the bed, 1 bounced off and banged his head, daddy rang the doctor and the doctor said, no more piglets bouncing on the bed

Variables

Now we want to look at the variables in the code and have a little fun with them. The variable here is x. What would happen if we changed the x to a y in line one? If we changed both x variables to y, would the output change again? Try it and see. What if we changed x to read RandomTurkeyVariable? Yes, I know, it's an awful name but my point is this – it doesn't matter what the variable is called. You don't have to use x or y – you can use anything you want.

Let's Create a while loop

Time to move on; let's have a look at another common loop, the while loop. Where the for loop usually stops after a set number of times, a while loop only stops when a certain condition has been met.

To test this out, type this code into the editor:

```
x=0

while x is not 8:

    x=x+1

    print (x)

print('done!')
```

This is what you will see:

```
1

2

3

4

5

6

7

8

done!
```

Ask the kids to explain what this code does, using 'variable' and 'loop'.

In this code, our variable is x. It begins at 0 and, on every run of the loop, it will increase by 1, as per the formula in the code of x=x+1. When it reaches 10, the condition that was set to finish the loop has been met and the loop has finished. The word, 'done!' is printed to show this.

Earlier, we ran a for loop; this time, it was a while loop. All loops can be very useful in computer programming because they help us to control how we progress through the code – 'done!' won't be printed until the condition is met and the loop is done running.

Why Syntax is Important

As we talked about earlier, syntax is just the grammar of the computer program and a computer can only execute a command if we provide it in a way that they can understand. One way that we can understand how important syntax is, type in the following code. We have taken the indent away from print x:

```
x=0
```

while x is not 8:

```
    x=x+1
```

```
print (x)
```

```
print('done!')
```

What happens when you remove the indent? Discuss what happens when you do this and understand that the indents underneath each while or for code line are used to define the loop boundaries. The loop won't execute or run any of the code underneath the line that has not been indented.

But, type this code in and see what happens:

```
x=0

while x is not 8:

    x=x+1

print (x)

print('done!')
```

The code won't work and an error message looking a little like this will be displayed:

```
File "<ipython-input-10-ebd4d8eb92d4>", line 5

print('done!')

    ^
```

IndentationError: unexpected indent

Python will, on occasion, attempt to help you see where the code is wrong by inserting a ∧ (caret symbol) into the error message. In this case, the error happened because print('done!) should not be indented – a classic syntax error and the computer is unable to understand the command.

Tip

If your computer program freezes or gets stuck, press on CTRL+C or click on the red square in the editor – the program will stop. To see what it will look like, type in this code and run it:

```
x=0

while x is not 8:

    print (x)

x=x+1
```

Why doesn't it work? Because the value in the variable, x, does not get to 8 inside the loop. This means it will keep on running and will continue to print 0s only.

How to Import a Library

To finish this chapter, we are going to look at how to turn the computer into a dice using a library. Type this code in:

```
from random import randint

x = randint(1,4)

print("dice roll:")

print(x)
```

We are importing a library called random and taking a method from it called randint. Random is a Python module type that provides us with many different functions to use. Here, randint(x, y) is a function provided by random that will take two parameters – these are the x and y variables. A random number is chosen in between x and y (inclusive). These variables can be set to whatever you want – we opted for 1, 6, because that is what is on a dice.

If we wanted lots of different functions from the random library, we would probably just type in:

```
import random
```

This would import the entire library and not just a method.

What does the code do? What other modifications could you make to the code? Play about with changing the smallest number and the largest numbers that may be produced, or decide that the dice will only be rolled if the number equals or is under four. It could look something like this:

```
from random import randint

roll=randint(1, 6)

print(roll)

if roll < 4 :

    repeat=roll

    print(roll)

else:

    print("You lost!")
```

Troubleshooting

If the code doesn't work, the most common types of error are in the parentheses () – the number of opening parentheses – (- must be matched by an equal number of closing parentheses -). Other common errors are in indents and colons – usually where they have been missed out.

- Every logic statement, such as the if, for, and while statements, must end with a colon

- A for loop will only work on the lines beneath them that have been correctly indented – make sure that the number of indents is only one greater than the loop.

Chapter Eight

Exploring Lists

Very often in computer programming, kids will come across words that they don't understand and will find a little intimidating. It is important, as they learn to program using Python, that they understand this – all problems can be split down into several smaller steps and they should be. This helps them to write code that is clean and understandable by others who may read it.

In this chapter, we will be looking at working with data, editing it and storing it. Data is just another way of saying 'information'.

The concepts we will look at are:

- **Data Types** – Python has many different data types, and as we learn more Python commands, we will learn what some of them are

- **Lists** – information or data in a certain order that we can change.

So, data. What does all this mean?

Let's Create a List

Creating a list in Python is very simple. All it requires is a list of items, each separated by a comma, in between a set of square bracket – []. Let's create one now by typing this into the editor:

```
myList = ['I', "don't", "like", "marmite", "on", "my", "toast"]
```

In computer programming, we call this a declaration and we have declared a variable called myList. In this list, we have placed some words and we defined the list using the square brackets. We can find out information about what's in the list plus we can change the data by using specific commands.

Let's see how to get information about our list.

We want to get some simple information – how long the list is, the first bit of stored data, the last, and what type the data is. To do that, we need to learn and understand a few basic commands.

The Length of the List

To find out what length our list is, we use the following command:

print (len(myList))

On your screen, you will see something similar to this:

>>> len(myList)

7

7 is the length of our list because it has 7 words in it.

List Indexing

Each item in a list has an index – this makes it easier to retrieve them. To find a specific item in the list, we need the index operator []. Let's say that we want the first bit of data; we would type in the command

myList[1]

What value is returned? Is it what you expected to see?

>>> print (myList[1])

don't

You will see the word, 'don't' on your screen – why? Have a play about, see if you can get the word, 'I' printed on the screen. Why do you think it didn't print when we asked for the first word?

Indexing in Python begins are 0, not 1. So, to get the first word, 'I', to print, you need to do this:

myList[0].

To help you, this is what indexing is like:

I | DON'T | LIKE | MARMITE | ON | MY | TOAST

0   1   2   3   4   5   6

So, given this, how would you search for the final word, or element, in this list? Try inputting

myList[7]

An error will appear. Although there are 7 items in the list, because indexing begins at 0, the seventh item is number 6. This will likely be quite confusing to start with but, once they get the hang of counting from 0 and not 1, it will all fall into place.

The Types of Data in Lists

Type the following into the editor:

type(myList)

On the screen, you should see this, or something similar:

>>> print (type(myList))

That isn't really what we wanted to know. What we want is to find out what the type of data or information is that the list is storing. I know – let's try this instead:

>>> print (type(myList[1]))

And this is what should appear

<class 'str'>

Ah, that's more like it! 'str' is short for 'strings', which are pieces of text. You can easily spot a string because it will be surrounded quote marks – double or single. **IMPORTANT NOTE** – the quote marks must match – if you start with a single quote, you must end with one; do NOT mix single and double quotes as you will get an error.

Look back over the commands we used before – you will see that all the entries for myList are enclosed in quote marks.

Lists, Integers, and Strings

How can we tell the difference between these three data types?

This is something that the kids can play about with and learn by defining at least two variables.

marmite = "I don't like marmite on my toast"

marmite2= ["I don't like marmite on my toast"]

Run the above two variables using two different commands on both of them – len and type. Compare the results to what we got from myList. What do they see? Let them have a play about, explore a little with variables of their own – the fun in programming is the ability to create their own examples on any strange and wonderful ideas they may have.

When the len command is used, this is what we see:

```
>>> print (len(marmite))

32

>>> print (len(marmite2))

1
```

And if the type command is used on each one:

```
>>> type(marmite)

<class 'str'>

>>> type(marmite2)

<class 'list'>
```

The point I am trying to make is that the variable called marmite is not a list; it is a string. Lists are defined with square brackets. The variable length is 32 – why? Because using the len function will count every character individually, including spaces. The list, marmite2, has just one element enclosed in the quote marks and that is why the length is just 1.

So, looking at the Python console, what other information do we see? Ask the kids to look at the numbers 1 and 32. Ask them to type the following into the editor:

```
type(1)
```

and then

```
type(32)
```

The result is an int – this tells us that the data is of an integer type. An integer is a whole number – it may be a negative number or a positive number, or it may be 0.

```
>>> type(32)

<class 'int'>
```

Extra Task

Ask the kids to get the first letter of the string called marmite. Tell them that it is much the same as getting information from a list and see if they can work out how to do it.

What they type in should be:

```
marmite[0]
```

What is the data type of that command?

It is a string and, as it happens, strings consist of lots of smaller strings.

Have a look at a few examples of getting different letters from the string:

```
>>> marmite[0]

I

>>> marmite[20]

e

>>> marmite[17]

m

>>> marmite[31]

s
```

This teaches the kids how data is stored in Python. We have looked at three different variable types lists, strings, and integers. Lists store data in a certain order and indexing begins at 0 – the last bit of data in the list is at a position numbered on less than the total length of the list.

Even the simplest of Python commands can store a whole lot of data! Don't get confused – go over things as much as you need to make sure you understand it.

Making Changes to Lists

What we have learned so far is:

- List indexes start at 0

- Attributes built into Python, such as length

Now we can turn our attention to methods and commands that can help us to make changes to our lists.

We'll go back to our original list, declared as:

myList = ["I", "do not", "like", "marmite", "in","my", "toast."]

First, we will add a couple of words to our list. Type in these two commands:

myList.insert(4,"or")

myList.insert(5,"jelly")

Now, to see our list contents again, we type:

myList

What happened here?

Ask them to type the command a few more times, using different words and numbers – what happens each time?

```
>>> myList.insert(4,"or")

>>> myList.insert(5,"jelly")

>>> myList
```

['I', 'don't', 'like', 'marmite', 'or', jelly, 'on', 'my', 'toast']

Do be verbal when teaching kids to use Python – it is far better than just having them tap away at the keyboard without really knowing what they are doing and why. When you talk about a piece of code verbally, the brain slows down and has the chance to work out what is going on.

Let's Look At Parameters

One of the more important things to learn is that, in the parentheses, we have two terms. Each one is known, in Python, as a parameter. The first one is used to define the location in terms of index where the second one will go. In our case, the second one does not need to be a string – lists can hold more than one variable type and they don't all need to be the same.

Remove a Parameter

We can also use the remove() command. This will take a parameter, which must the element or entry value we want removed. When we talk of a value, we talk of the information that each entry in the list stores.

Let's start by copying our list; type this:

```
testList=myList
```

Now we want to remove an entry – the word 'don't' – from our testList. The command should look like

```
testList.remove()
```

102

And, as we said earlier, it will have a parameter – if we don't give it one, it won't know what to remove. The entire command should look like this:

>>> testList.remove("don't")

>>> testList

And the result will be:

['I', 'like', 'marmite', 'or', jelly, 'on', 'my', 'toast']

>>>

At this point, we should take some time to talk about one of the most important bits of the syntax:

Parentheses and Brackets

We learned that an array can have features, such as indexing, and attributes, such as length, built into them. You should have notice one thing – some commands have brackets [] and some require parentheses (). This is syntax, how the Python language uses spacing and punctuation as a form of organization – not just for code flow, but for operational purposes too.

Generally speaking, brackets are used as an indication that we are accessing or creating data. Go back to when we declared the myList variable – that is an example of data creation, while an example of data access is myList[0] – when we asked for the first bit of data in our list.

Questions

1. When you create a variable, how do you know it is not a list?

2. What would happen if you used parentheses and not brackets to create lists?

3. How do we gain access to a specific index in any list?

Back to parameters – we know that these are provided to Python commands, although not all commands need them. Any parameter must be enclosed in parentheses.

Questions

1. What are parameters?

2. What would happen if we used brackets and not parentheses when we use a command that modifies a list, such as remove or insert?

3. Why is the difference between using parentheses and brackets important?

Let's discuss that last question for a moment. It is one of the most important of all Python concepts because it takes away the confusion between asking for some information or providing commands. For example:

listA=[2,3,4,5]

All of the entries are numbers.

If there wasn't any difference between parentheses and brackets, a command such as

remove(2)

would cause confusion – we wouldn't know if were removing the value of 2, which is indexed at 0, or 4, indexed at 2.

Summary

We have learned about variables and ways they can be manipulated in Python and that lists enable us to use parameters to access specific data. We also learned some more important information about Python syntax.

Chapter Nine

The Benefits of Learning to Code

Coding is now one of the most important trends in education and kids the world over are learning how to code. While not every child will go on to become a programmer, learning to code does offer several benefits.

Learning Computational and Computer Skills

When kids learn code writing, they develop a couple of very important skills – cognitive and how to solve problems the same way a computer does. Coding involves pattern recognition, presentation of problems in ways that involve breaking them down into smaller parts and dealing with each part individually. Aside from learning how to code, children learn how to think in other situations to help solve problems.

It's the New 'Literacy'

The world our children are growing up is in very different to the one we grew up in. Their lives revolve around cell phones, computers, social media and more. Even the latest toys are digital, with some even having their own programming. However, knowing how to use all this technology is one thing; learning what goes into it is another thing entirely. With coding, children learn what makes their social media or computers tick, how they are controlled. Kids of today will grow up in a digital, technological world and they need to understand how it all works.

It Teaches Kids How to Solve Problems

Learning to code involves breaking one problem into several smaller ones and this can apply to any problem in the real world. As well as a subject that is relevant to the future of our job market, coding also teaches children about the development of skills in different areas – math, statistics, geometry, data analysis, trigonometry, and much more – all important areas, especially in problem solving.

It Brings Job Opportunities

For kids to stand a chance in an ever-evolving economy, their skill set must be varied and comprehensive and one subject that they must learn is technology. In the future, kids that can't code will be seen exactly the same as kids that can't read. Most of our future jobs will require some kind of computer skills an those who can code will have the best chance at employment.

Important Skills

The fact that the future will revolve almost entirely around technology means that there will be a much higher requirement for people who can code. There is a firm belief that those who can write compute programs will be able to earn very well in the future and even if a job doesn't need the use of computers, it will still require coding skills. As well, children also learn how to communicate, how to think critically, how to free their creativity and more when they learn how to code.

Coding Means Creative

Kids are far more creative in their thinking than most adults are, and with coding revolving around an endless need to find different code variations and solutions should give them the motivation they need to release their creative sides. Those that can learn to code quickly will immediately spot the big connection between writing code and telling a story – they both have patterns much the same. This can lead to them being more successful in both writing and in speaking in public.

Avoiding Problems and Learning Perseverance

Coding teaches kids about problem handling and how to anticipate problems and errors. Learning to write the code correctly can stop a program crashing. And what happens if what they write doesn't work as it should? It teaches them to find out what has gone wrong, why it went wrong, and how to put it right.

It isn't an accident that coding has grown in popularity and it's now becoming common knowledge that kids should learn to code. After all, they are the next generation and they will need these skills to get on in life, not just in employment, but in dealing with everything real life will throw their way.

It Improves Collaboration Skills

All kids have the ability to learn anything and all kids have the ability to learn how to write computer code. And they can learn that alongside other people, regardless of gender, race, background, beliefs, etc. Kids meet new kids all the time and they learn how to get on with, to collaborate with them – where coding is concerned, they are all learning in an environment of a shared interest in technology. Classrooms, playgrounds, and any other environment where the children are present in person, all teach the children how to collaborate face to face. And when kids learn online, they also have the ability to grow, asking questions of one another, working on collaborative problem solving and creating things together. Games such as Minecraft are excellent examples – they offer many different educational benefits including participation, collaboration and coding together with people from all over the world.

It Improves Communication Skills

If there is one skill we all need in life, it is communication. Kids must learn how to communicate throughout their early years, school years, working years, and life in general. If they can communicate a complex problem, solution, or idea in a simple way, they have a much better chance of being successful in anything they do, no matter what direction life takes them in. By learning how to write code, kids can learn the skill of communication with one of the simplest audiences possible – the computer. Because it teaches them how to break each problem down into smaller ones, and because it teaches them how to rearrange those smaller problems in a way that the computer understands, it teaches them how to communicate in the easiest possible way – that should give them the confidence they need to communicate with anyone, anywhere.

Conclusion

Coding is all around us. We interact with it on a daily basis, but do any of us really take time to consider how it all works? Probably not.

Children are curious creatures by nature, and it is always good to foster this curiosity therefore when they start to take in interest in how things such as computers, smartphones, stoplights or automatic tills work, wouldn't it be great to be able to foster this curiosity by giving them answers? Or even better, letting them find out for themselves with some adult help?

Teaching a young child how to code sounds complicated, especially when we as adults don't always understand it, but all we need to do is take it right back to basics. A good place to start is to get them interested in coding by identifying those objects that use code which we encounter every day and start them thinking about how it works.

Really, what is coding? It is simply a set of instructions that tell a computer what to do. Yes, there are lots of programming languages, but you don't have to concern yourself (or your child) with this in the beginning. Once they are beginning to code, it is helpful to know a little bit about them and maybe focus on one specific one once they have mastered the block-based coding and are ready to move on but how you choose this can be dependent upon what their interests are. For example, if they are interested in robotics, then finding a website or program that teaches Arduino may be preferable. If their interest lies in building websites, then look for courses that teach HTML or CSS. If they have an interest in things such as YouTube, Spotify or Instagram, then maybe learning Python would be valuable.

Your child may not ever want to work with computers, but who knows what we want to do when we are an adult, really? How many of us actually have the job we said we wanted to do when we were six years old? My son's dream job changes every day. One day he wants to drive an ambulance, the next day he wants to be a police officer, the day after that he wants to build video games, and so it goes on. Whatever job they want to do in the future – whether they know what that is now or not – doesn't matter. Coding will still be important when they are at an age to start a career. If we look at how far technology has come in the last thirty years since I was a child, how much will it change in the next ten, twenty, or thirty years? I – and many experts – believe that technology is going to be in a lot of job sectors, so having even just a basic understanding can put your child ahead of others. The world is changing, and I believe what we teach our child needs to change to match this.

So you want to teach your child to code? The first step is to start doing some offline games, away from the computer. Start laying the foundation by slowly introducing some of these basic coding concepts to children, such as breaking down instructions, giving instructions in a methodical way, giving directions, deciphering codes, recognizing, and developing patterns.

Many children are kinetic learners and retain information far easier if they have hands-on experience with concepts, therefore, offline games are very important even if to us, as adults, they seem basic and far removed from the idea we envision when we think of computer coding.

These offline coding activities can be added into everyday routines. Even in a school setting, they can be incorporated into Literacy, Mathematics, and even PE lessons.

At home, you can just be playing fun activities with your child. They don't even have to know they are doing anything related to coding.

The idea of the offline games is not only to get children away from the computer to teach the basic concepts but also to get them to think logically, learn to problem solve, work collaboratively as well as to learn patience, determination, and resilience. All skills that are valuable throughout life, not just for coding, can be learned through these fun games.

Games such as mazes, treasure hunts, deciphering codes, sequencing pictures, and events, and writing instructions can all help with these important skills.

Once your child is ready to code on a computer, then look at different resources. Consider whether it is worth paying a subscription or whether just free apps and websites will suffice. I would always recommend going for free websites such as Scratch to learn block-based coding before moving on to paid subscriptions as you can find out if your child has an interest in them or not. Sometimes in a home environment, children prefer toys and apps over one specific website, so it may be worth looking into these rather than a website subscription.

In a school environment paid subscriptions are probably the way forward but look for ones with lifetime membership or school discounts so that you can get the most benefit for the least amount of money but also choose one that is suitable for the age and ability you are teaching and what you want your students to learn.

Remember, however, – and wherever – you are teaching, foster a good learning environment. Trial and error is all part of learning when it comes to coding. Whether children can spot mistakes can be a good indicator of progression, make sure you have a positive attitude that accepts that mistakes happen, and it's okay – in fact, it is beneficial because we can learn from those mistakes.

Children like it when adults make mistakes, so when you know that they have a good understanding of what you are teaching them, then you can make mistakes too. Maybe you program a robot incorrectly, or maybe your maze directions sends them to a lava pit instead of a sweet spot. Does your child notice this and pick up on it?

Maybe you give them instructions in the wrong order, or you miss out a step when baking. Let them correct you. Not only is it fun for them but also it helps them to learn.

In a classroom environment, try to adopt a 'collaborative' way or working; encourage children to support one another and work as a team, supporting each other to correct mistakes together rather than making negative comments to those that get it wrong.

Children work better in pairs, and so at least in the beginning, it can be beneficial to pair children up so that they can bounce ideas off each other and have discussions about why they think something works in a certain way or how they think a problem can be solved. It can give children far more confidence if they are paired up rather than being left to their own devices and if one person isn't quite sure about something, the other person may understand it better. Likewise, if neither of them understands the activity, they may be more inclined to speak up rather than become lost or frustrated.

If you are working at home with your child, then work together rather than leaving them to play by themselves. If possible involve other family members, too.

Don't forget; when you work through the practical examples in the book, do it slowly. There is no need to rush through it; indeed, if you do, the kids probably won't understand it. And if they don't, it's a waste of your time and theirs. Take it slowly, work through each concept, one at a time, and do not move on until they understand what they have done and why.

Finally, make it FUN! Coding doesn't have to be a boring, dry, academic subject. It can be taken outside. It can be done via games.

It can be done on apps. The only limitation is your imagination! Foster that creativity in your children by being creative yourself. Find different resources, adapt the games and activities included in this book and let your imagination run wild!

Resources

How to say 'Hello World' in different programming languages

https://learn.excelwithbusiness.com/blog/post/web-design/say-hello-world-in-28-different-programming-languages

Hour Of Code activities for various ages and abilities

https://code.org/learn

Scratch

https://scratch.mit.edu/

Tynker

https://www.tynker.com/

Bitsbox

https://bitsbox.com/

Codakid

https://codakid.com/

Codeacademy

https://www.codecademy.com/

Treehouse

https://teamtreehouse.com/

Udemy

https://www.udemy.com/topic/coding-for-kids/

List of Coding Books Aimed At Children

https://www.codemom.ai/2017/05/best-coding-books-for-kids/

https://www.readbrightly.com/childrens-books-to-introduce-coding/

Coding Summer Camps

https://www.rivalearning.com/

https://www.codecamp.co.uk/

https://funtechsummercamps.com/

Made in the USA
Monee, IL
04 December 2019